SQL COMPUTER PROGRAMMING FOR BEGINNERS

THE ULTIMATE GUIDE TO LEARN SQL PROGRAMMING BASICS, SQL LANGUAGES, QUERIES AND PRACTICE PROBLEMS, SQL SERVER AND DATABASE, CODING LANGUAGES FOR BEGINNERS.

Introduction

Network programs are larger and more flexible. In many cases, the fundamental scheme of operations is mainly a mix of scripts that handle the command of a database.

Due to the variety of languages and pre-existing sources, the method to "talk" between one another may usually be challenging and complicated, fortunately for us, the presence of requirements that permit us to do the typical methods by way of a wide spread form can make this particular perplexing task even more simple.

That is what Structured Query Language (SQL) is based on, that typically is only a worldwide common language of interaction within databases. That is precisely why, the Structured Query Language (SQL) is really a standardized language which allows most people to apply some language e.g. PHP or ASP, in conjunction with any particular database e.g. MySQL, MS Access, SQL Server.

IBM made SQL throughout the1970's; in the novice, it had been named SEQUEL (Structure English Query

Language). Years later, Oracle and Microsoft also began with the use of SEQUEL.

The global recognition grew after which the word SEQUEL was transformed. In 1986, the word SEQUEL was standardized by the American National Standards Institute (ANSI) to SQL. In other words, they ditched the earth "English" from the word.

Until this morning, there are plenty of owners that decline to reference it as SQL, to these individuals; SEQUEL definitely may be the proper rap because of this standardized data source language. SQL has also been revised in 1989 and 1992. Since then, SQL has undergone many revisions to improve their standardization.

SQL is certainly a worldwide-standardized vocabulary, but that doesn't imply that is very similar for every repository. Truth be told, many databases execute particular functions, which will not generally run in others.

That is the explanation why every business that gives database solutions, for example Oracle and Microsoft, have their own certification process ensuring that people who takes the certification examination are really well prepared and understand the differences in between the different types of SQL. Their knowledge is concentrating on their own distinctive certain variant of SQL.

SQL is not simply relevant due to the ability to standardize a usually confusing language; it offers two other special characteristics. On a single hand, it actually is tremendously adaptable and powerful. On the opposite hand, it is really accessible which makes it much easier to master.

There are lots of databases items that support SQL, nonetheless, two of the largest and most popular are Microsoft SQL server and Oracle website.

Each company that provides database product has their own path to be an "expert". For instance, Microsoft offers an assortment of accreditation to guarantee that each Microsoft SQL Certified meets their criteria. Oracle does exactly the same thing with their Certification process.

1. Basic SQL Commands

Listed in this chapter are all of the various commands that you can use in SQL. The more basic commands are at the beginning of the chapter whereas the more advanced commands will be found further on down the chapter. The command name will be listed along with how it can be used and how to properly use it with the syntax included. Operators and clauses along with keywords will be mentioned after the basic commands. Examples will be shown on how to properly use each command.

Commands

CREATE DATABASE

In order to create your own database, you would use the following syntax as shown below.

CREATE DATABASE database_name

CREATE TABLE

After you create your database, you want to start creating tables to be entered into the database as well.

The CREATE TABLE command can be used as shown below.

CREATE TABLE table_name

(column_name1 data_type,

column_name2 data_type,

column_name3 data_type,);

Here is an example:

CREATE TABLE Individuals

(Id number(20),

Last varchar (255)

First varchar (255)

Address varchar (255)

City varchar (255));

The result would give you a table of Individuals with their information sorted out by their first and last name, their address, and the city that they are located in. The

Id at the top stands for their ID number that would be entered in as a number. The ID column is able to hold a number of up to 20 digits.

INSERT

After you have your database and your tables all set up, you may find yourself needing to add another row into an existing table. In order to do this without setting up a completely new table, you can use the INSERT INTO command. The syntax is as shown below.

INSERT INTO table_name

VALUES (value1, value2, value3);

The following syntax will only be specific to the values of a column. It won't be able to specify any of the column names. In the instance that you want to specify the column values along with their names as well, you can use the following syntax as shown below.

INSERT INTO table_name

(column_1, column_2, column_3)

VALUES (value1, value2, value3)

If you wanted to be able to insert a new row into the table, it would be done using a similar syntax as shown below.

INSERT INTO table_name

VALUES ('insert various row information here') example: (3 such as 'row 3', 'Williams such as last name', 'Travis such as first name')

This will allow you to be able to insert multiple amounts of various data into different rows at the same time.

To be able to insert data into specific columns, you can use the following syntax shown below.

INSERT INTO Individuals

(Id, Last, First)

VALUES (5, 'Thompson', 'Jessica')

This would enter the information into row 5 and the column of the last name the name "Thompson" would be entered. Then the following name "Jessica" would be entered into the first name column.

Now that we have thoroughly covered the first few basic commands associated with the CREATE type commands of CRUD, it's now time to move on to the next type of commands of the acronym. The next step would be to query or read your data that you have created and inserted into your database. The next command will show you how to easily and specifically retrieve information from your database.

SELECT

In order to be able to query and read data in your database, you want to be able to select whatever data you want to be retrieved back to you. This is where the SELECT command comes into use. The command can be formed as shown in the syntax shown below.

SELECT columns

FROM tables

[JOIN joins]

WHERE search_condition]

[GROUP BY grouping_columns]

[HAVING search_condition]

```
[ORDER BY sort_columns];
```

This is a more complex syntax that can be used for a very specific search. The operators, clauses and keywords mentioned in the syntax will be introduced after the basic commands are presented. This is a syntax that you can come back to once you thoroughly understand how to use each part.

In order to retrieve a single column from a table, the following syntax can be used as shown below.

```
SELECT column
FROM table;
```

In order to retrieve multiple columns from a table, use the following syntax shown below.

```
SELECT columns
FROM table;
```

In order to retrieve all columns from a table, you are selecting the table as a whole since you are not wanting one or more columns over the others. In order to select a table, the keyword "FROM" comes into use. Use the following syntax as shown below.

```
SELECT * FROM table;
```

Just how we selected multiple columns from a table earlier, the same is applied as shown below. For instance, say you have a table named "Clients" and you want to search your clients by their first and last name. You would use the syntax as shown below.

SELECT Last, First

FROM Clients

Here is another example of how you would use the SELECT command to pull up a whole table instead of specified columns of a table. Let's say you just wanted to search your client list how it is in the database without searching clients by their first or last name. You would use the syntax shown below.

SELECT * FROM Clients

Now that we have covered the create and read type commands, the next commands will be update as a part of the CRUD commands. Now that you understand how to create and read the data that you enter into your database and tables, the next step that you will need to do is to be able to update the data that you've entered.

UPDATE

When you need to update data that exists in a table, you can use the UPDATE command in order to do so. It can be used as shown in the syntax below.

UPDATE table_name

SET column1=value, column2=value, column3=value

[WHERE search_condition];

Without properly placing the WHERE clause, all of the data or the improper data will be updated by the command. Listed below is another way to properly use the WHERE clause in the UPDATE command as an example of a specific table with specific data.

UPDATE Clients

(SET First= 'Jason'

City= 'Rochester'

WHERE Last= 'Knight');

This example would add in the first name and city that the client lives in by searching for his last name. Of course, you can be more specific with the WHERE clause as you might have plenty of clients in a chart with the same last name. You could use the WHERE clause to search for other conditions in a table to make sure your results will be specific and sure.

Now that you understand how to not only create and read data in a database but now you understand how to update it as well. The last step of "CRUD" is delete. There are several more ways to delete information in SQL than you would think. The following commands listed will be different ways that you can delete data to your own needs or preference.

DELETE

When you find yourself needing to delete rows in a table, the DELETE command can be used in order to do so. To properly use it, follow the syntax shown below.

DELETE FROM table_name

[WHERE search_condition];

Here, the search condition would be used to fill in the name or placement of the row. If the WHERE clause is improperly used with the DELETE command, all of the records will be deleted as a result.

When you want to be able to remove just one individual row from your table, you can use the following syntax example as shown below.

```
DELETE FROM Clients

WHERE Last= 'Johnson'

AND First= 'Sarah';
```

Here, the AND keyword is used as well as the WHERE clause. The AND keyword will be presented more in depth later on. Here, you can see that it is used to add a more specific search to aid the deletion process of an individual in the Clients table. The example would simply and only remove that one client with that first and last name. If you had other clients with the same name, this is where more specific identification can be used such as a unique ID number for your clients in your database.

In the case that you want to be able to delete all the rows in a table, you can use the following syntax as shown below.

```
DELETE * FROM table_name;
```

DROP

The DROP command can be used in order to delete an index that is contained in a table. The DROP command can also be used to delete a database or a table. Indexes can be created in order to speed up a search in your database by making your tables more defined. They won't be visible to those who view the table, only those who search for the table. Shown below is a syntax on how to properly use the DROP command when deleting an index. There are four variations for the syntax depending on what platform you are using SQL on.

Access:

DROP INDEX index_name

MS SQL Server:

DROP INDEX

table_name.index_name

Oracle:

DROP INDEX index_name

MySQL:

ALTER TABLE table_name

DROP INDEX index_name

When you want to be able to delete a table in your database, you can use the DROP TABLE command in order to do so. The syntax is properly shown below.

How to use the DROP TABLE command:

DROP TABLE table_name

When you want to be able to delete the whole database itself, you can use the DROP DATABASE command in order to do so. The proper syntax is shown below.

How to use the DROP DATABASE command:

DROP DATABASE database_name

TRUNCATE

The TRUNCATE command can be used whenever you want to delete data that is already contained in a table without removing the whole table itself. This can be useful for times when you want to start fresh without completely start over in your table. In order to properly use the TRUNCATE command, the syntax is shown below.

```
TRUNCATE TABLE table_name
```

That then completes the four categories of commands that "CRUD" stands for. The following syntaxes will be of operators, clauses and keywords that can be used in commands. Some of them have already been shown in the commands listed. These extras can add precise work to your commands and be quite useful.

Operators and Clauses

AND

When you want to look a client or anything in your table, you can use the AND operator to make the search more specific. If you were looking up a client, this could be used to look the individual up by their first AND last name. If you were looking for a Garrett Lee in your database, you would use the following syntax in order to use the AND operator to do so.

```
SELECT * FROM Clients
```

WHERE First= 'Garrett'

AND Last= 'Lee'

OR

This operator is similar to the AND operator. If you wanted to be able to find two different kinds of clients in your database by their first OR last name, you could use the following syntax as shown below.

SELECT * FROM Clients

WHERE First= 'John'

OR Last= 'Thomas'

This would be able to bring up any client in your database with either the first name of John or the last name of Thomas. Of course, you could use this operator in whatever way you wanted to in order to bring up more precise results.

AND/OR

This operator can be used in order to filter your records using more than one condition. The AND and OR operators can be quite useful by themselves but they become even more useful when combined together in order to refine your search. The AND operator will display two records due to the two specific conditions if the data search applies to both. When a record is adequate to either the first or second condition, the OR operator will display the more specific results. The syntax is example is shown below.

```
SELECT * FROM Clients

WHERE Last= 'Jones'

AND (First= 'Carl' OR First= 'Mark')
```

By combining these commands together, the results will select individuals that have the same last name that is specified. This will pick up on individuals that have the last name that is equal to the last name "Jones" and the first names of either "Carl" or "Mark".

NOT

This operator can be used in order to rule by one condition when searching your database. This operator is used as a clause with the SELECT command. The proper syntax is shown below.

```
SELECT * First, Last, State
FROM Clients
WHERE NOT (State = 'AK');
```

The results would bring up clients by their first and last name along with the state that they lived in. It would bring up all clients except for the ones that live in Alaska. Of course, you could add more states than just one for your search.

WHERE

The WHERE clause has been shown in previous commands in order to be specific to the use of the command. It is very important where you place the WHERE clause. In order to make sure you have a good idea of how to properly use it, included below are two syntaxes that are shown in correct and incorrect formats along with the initial syntax that should be used.

```
SELECT column_names
FROM table_name
WHERE test_column operator value;
```

Say you want to retrieve clients from a city:

SELECT * FROM Clients

WHERE City= 'Portland'

How to use WHERE clause with text and numeric values:

Correct:

SELECT * FROM Clients

[WHERE First='Amanda']

Incorrect:

SELECT * FROM Clients

(WHERE First=Amanda)

Correct:

SELECT * FROM Clients

WHERE Year=1985

Incorrect:

SELECT * FROM Clients

WHERE Year= '1985'

GROUP BY

This operator can be used with other commands in order to group the result of one or more columns of a table. The proper syntax use is shown below.

SELECT column_name

Aggregate_function (column_name)

FROM table_name

WHERE column_name operator value

GROUP BY column_name

This operator can also be used in order to find the total sum that a client has purchased from you in the case that you are a business owner that keeps your records in your database. A proper syntax in order to use this is shown below.

SELECT Clients, SUM (Orders Purchased)

FROM Products

GROUP BY Clients

This would bring up how much an individual had purchased from you by pulling up the orders that had been purchased from the products.

In order to bring up more than one column, you can use the syntax example below:

SELECT Clients, Date, SUM (Orders Purchased)

FROM Products

GROUP BY Clients, Date

This would bring up a column for each of the sums according to the clients and the date as well.

ORDER BY

Similar to the GROUP BY operator, the ORDER BY keyword is not much different. It will pull up your results in a specific order depending on what you decide to put in for your benefit. By default, your data that you retrieve will come back to you in ascending order. In the case that you wanted it to come back in a descending order, you would use the keyword 'DESC'. You can use this keyword in the following syntax example shown below.

```
SELECT column_names
FROM table_name
ORDER BY sort_columns [ASC | DESC];
```

In order to sort multiple columns, the following syntax example can be used:

```
SELECT column_names
FROM table_name
ORDER BY
sort_column1 [ASC | DESC],
sort_column2 [ASC | DESC],
sort_column3 [ASC | DESC];
```

In order to sort by column positions in relevance:

```
SELECT column_names
FROM table_name
ORDER BY
sort_number1 [ASC | DESC],
sort_number2 [ASC | DESC],
sort_number3 [ASC | DESC];
```

In order to sort by order in descending order:

SELECT * FROM Clients

ORDER BY Last name DESC

The results would bring up data of your clients by their last name from Z to A instead of alphabetical order. In the case of numbers, it would bring up the lowest numbers up to the highest numbers.

DISTINCT

In the event that you need to eliminate any duplicate rows, you can do this by using the DISTINCT keyword to do so. You can use this keyword in the following syntax shown below.

SELECT DISTINCT column_names

FROM table_name

You can also combine the SELECT command with the DISTINCT keyword. If you wanted to be able to find clients from a specific city, you could use the following syntax example shown below.

SELECT DISTINCT New York City

From Clients

This will bring up all the clients in your database that live specifically in New York City.

2. SQL Functions

SQL count function

The COUNT() function is used to return the number of rows that meets the given condition.

Here's the syntax:

In this statement, the expression can refer to an arithmetic operation or column name. You can also specify (*) if you want to calculate the total records stored in the table.

The examples in this section will use the data in SALES_REP table:

To perform a simple count operation like calculating how many rows are in the SALES_REP table, you will enter:

```
SELECT COUNT(EMP_NAME)

FROM SALES_REP;
```

Here's the result:

You can also use (*) instead of specifying a column name:

```
SELECT COUNT(EMP_NAME)

FROM SALES_REP;
```

This statement will produce the same result because the EMP_NAME field has no NULL value. Assuming, however, that one of the fields in the EMP_NAME contains a NULL value, this would not be included in the statement that specifies EMP_NAME but will be included in the COUNT() result if you use the * symbol as parameter.

You can also use the COUNT function with the GROUP by clause. For example, if you want to calculate the number of records for every branch, you can enter this statement:

```
SELECT BRANCH, COUNT(*) FROM SALES_REP

GROUP BY BRANCH;
```

This would be the output:

The COUNT() function can be used with DISTINCT to find the number of distinct entries. For instance, if you want to know how many distinct branches are saved in the SALES_REP table, you will enter this statement:

SELECT COUNT (DISTINCT BRANCH)

FROM SALES_REP;

It will produce this result:

SQL AVG Function

The AVG() function calculates the average value of columns with numeric data type.

Here is the syntax:

In the above statement, the expression can refer to an arithmetic operation or to a column name. Arithmetic operations can take single or multiple columns.

The examples in this section will use the SALES_REP table with this data:

In the first example, you will use the AVG() function to calculate the average sales amount. You can enter this statement:

SELECT AVG(Sales) FROM Sales_Rep;

Here's the result:

The figure 6245.500000 is the average of all sales data in the Sales_Rep table and it is computed by adding the Sales field and dividing the result by the number of records which, in this example, is 10 rows.

The AVG() function can be used in arithmetic operations. For example, assuming that sales tax is 6.6% of sales, you can use this statement to calculate the average sales tax figure:

SELECT AVG(Sales*.066) FROM Sales_Rep;

Here's the result:

To obtain the result, SQL had to calculate the result of the arithmetic operation 'Sales *.o66' before applying the AVG function.

You can combine the AVG() function with the GROUP BY clause to get the average figure for a specified grouping. For example, assume that you want to calculate the average sales for each branch, you can enter this statement:

```
SELECT Branch, AVG(Sales) FROM Sales_Rep
GROUP BY Branch;
```

Here's the result:

SQL ROUND Function

The ROUND() function is used to round a number to a given number of decimals or precision.

This is the syntax for SQL ROUND() function:

```
ROUND (expression, [decimal place])
```

In the above statement, the decimal place specifies the number of decimal points that will be returned. If you specify a negative number, it will round off the digit on the left of the decimal point. For instance, specifying -1 will round off the number to the nearest tens.

The examples on this section will use the Student_Grade table with the following data:

ID	Name	Grade
1	Jack Knight	87.6498
2	Daisy Poult	98.4359
3	James McDuff	97.7853
4	Alicia Stone	89.9753

Assuming that you want to round off the grades to the nearest tenths, you can enter this statement:

SELECT Name, ROUND (Grade, 1) Rounded_Grade
FROM Student_Grade;

This would be the result:

Assuming that you want to round the grades to the nearest tens, you will use a negative parameter for the ROUND() function:

```
SELECT Name, ROUND (Grade, -1) Rounded_Grade
FROM Student_Grade;
```

Here's the result:

SQL SUM Function

The SUM() function is used to return the total for an expression.

Here's the syntax for the SUM() function:

The expression parameter can refer to an arithmetic operation or a column name. Arithmetic operations may include one or more columns.

Likewise, there can be more than one column in the SELECT statement in addition to the column specified in the SUM() function. These columns should also form part of the GROUP BY clause. Here's the syntax:

For the examples in this section, you will use the SALES_REP table with the following data:

To calculate the total of all sales from the Sales_Rep, table, you will enter this statement:

```
SELECT SUM(Sales) FROM Sales_Rep;
```

This would be the result:

The figure 62455.00 represents the total of all entries in the Sales column.

To illustrate how you can use an arithmetic operation as an argument in the SUM() function, assume that you have to apply a sales tax of 6.6% on the sales figure. Here's the statement to obtain the total sales tax:

SELECT SUM(Sales*.066) FROM Sales_Rep;

You will get the following result:

In this example, you will combine the SUM() function and the GROUP BY clause to calculate the total sales for each branch. You can use this statement:

SELECT Branch, SUM(Sales) FROM Sales_Rep

GROUP BY Branch;

SQL MAX() Function

The MAX() function is used to obtain the largest value in a given expression.

Here's the syntax:

SELECT MAX (<expression>)

FROM table_name;

The expression parameter can be an arithmetic operation or a column name. Arithmetic operations can have multiple columns.

The SELECT statement can have one or more columns besides the column specified in the MAX() function. If this is the case, these columns will have to form part of the GROUP BY clause.

The syntax would be:

SELECT column1, column2, ... "columnN", MAX (<expression>)

FROM table_name;

GROUP BY column1, column2, ... "columnN";

To demonstrate, you will use the table Sales_Rep with this data:

To get the highest sales amount, you will enter this statement:

SELECT MAX(Sales) FROM Sales_Rep;

Here's the result:

To illustrate how the MAX() function is applied to an arithmetic operation, assume that you have to compute a sales tax of 6.6% on the sales figure. To get the highest sales tax figure, you will use this statement;

SELECT MAX(Sales*0.066) FROM Sales_Rep;

Here is the output:

You can combine the MAX() function with the GROUP BY clause to obtain the maximum sales value per branch. You will have to enter this statement:

SELECT Branch, MAX(Sales) FROM Sales_Rep GROUP BY Branch;

SQL MIN() Function

The MIN() function is used to obtain the lowest value in a given expression.

Here's the syntax:

SELECT MIN(<expression>)

FROM table_name;

The expression parameter can be an arithmetic operation or a column name. Arithmetic operations can also have several columns.

The SELECT statement can have one or several columns besides the column specified in the MIN() function. If this is the case, these columns will have to form part of the GROUP BY clause.

The syntax would be:

SELECT column1, column2, ... "columnN", MIN (<expression>)

FROM table_name;

GROUP BY column1, column2, ... "columnN";

To demonstrate how the MIN() function is used in SQL, you will use the Sales_Rep table with the following data:

To get the lowest sales amount, you can use this statement:

SELECT MIN(Sales) FROM Sales_Rep;

The output would be:

To demonstrate how the MIN() function is used on arithmetic operations, assume that you have to compute a sales tax of 6.6% on the sales figure. To get the lowest sales tax figure, you will use this statement;

SELECT MIN(Sales*0.066) FROM Sales_Rep;

Here's the output:

You can also use the MIN() function with the GROUP BY clause to calculate the minimum sales value per branch. You will have to enter this statement:

SELECT Branch, MIN(Sales) FROM Sales_Rep GROUP BY Branch.

3. Data Manipulation

DML (Data Manipulation Language) is the aspect of SQL that helps you to perform changes within a database. Through DML, you can fill tables with new information, update old tables, and remove unnecessary data from any table.

How to Populate a Table with New Information

You can complete this process in two ways: (1) enter the new data manually or (2) use computer programs to enter the data automatically. Manual data population refers to entering new data using a keyboard. Automated data population, on the other hand, refers to loading data from an outside source (e.g. a different database) and transferring it into the preferred database.

When entering new data, different factors can influence the type and quantity of data you can work with. Here are the main factors you have to consider: current constraints, the table's physical size, and the columns' length.

Important Note: You can run SQL statements without worrying about lowercase or uppercase characters. However, data is extremely case-sensitive. For instance, if you entered the data into a database using uppercase characters, you should use uppercase characters when referencing that data. The examples given below use uppercase and lowercase characters just to prove that this factor cannot influence the result.

How to Insert Data

You should use INSERT command to insert data into an existing table. This command has several options; check the syntax below:

With this syntax, you should specify each column in the list named VALUES. As you can see, the values in this list are separated by commas. You should use quotation marks to enclose the values you want to insert, particularly if you are working with date/time and character data types. You don't have to use quotation marks for NULL values or numeric data. Each column within the table should contain a value.

In the example below, you will insert a record into a table named "PRODUCTS_TBL."

The table's current structure:

Use this INSERT statement:

For this example, you inserted three values into a table that has three columns. The values you inserted follow the arrangement of columns within the table. Two of the values are enclosed with quotation marks because their columns are of the character type. The final value (i.e. cost) is a number data type: quotation marks are optional.

How to Insert Data into Specific Columns

You may insert data into certain columns. For example, let's assume that you need to insert the values for your employee except his pager number. In this case, you should determine a VALUES list and a column list while running the INSERT statement. Here's a screenshot of the values you may use:

When inserting values into specific columns, here is the syntax you should use:

In the example below, you'll insert values into specific columns inside a table named ORDERS_TBL. This is the table's current structure:

Let's say you used this INSERT statement:

In this INSERT statement, you specified a list of columns by enclosing the columns' names in parentheses. Also, the column list must be entered after the table's name. You have specified the columns that you need. Basically, you excluded the column named ORD_DATE.

If you'll check the table definition, you'll see that ORD_DATE is an independent column: it doesn't need any data from the table. This column doesn't require information since you didn't specify NOT NULL in the definition for the table. The NOT NULL statement says that the column accepts NULL values. Moreover, the array of values should follow the arrangement of the columns.

How to Insert Data from a Different Table

You can accomplish this by combining two SQL statements: INSERT and SELECT. Here's the syntax you should follow:

This syntax has new keywords: FROM, WHERE, and SELECT. Let's discuss them one by one. FROM is a part of the database query that determines the location of the needed data. This part should contain the name of table/s. WHERE, another part of the database query, applies conditions to improve the search results. Here's a sample condition: WHERE PRODUCT = 'CAR.' Lastly, SELECT is the primary statement used to begin the SQL query.

Important Note: "Applying a condition" means adding criteria on the information influenced by an SQL command.

How to Insert NULL Values

Inserting NULL values into an existing table is easy and simple. Why would you add this kind of value into your tables or databases? Well, you need to insert NULL values into a column if you don't know the specific value that should be placed there. For example, not every individual owns a cellphone, so it is imprecise to insert a wrong cellphone number. You can use the word NULL to insert null values into your desired column. Here's the syntax:

How to Update Data

You can use the UPDATE statement to modify data. This SQL statement doesn't add or delete records – it simply updates the data inside the table/s you are working on. In general, UPDATE is used to modify tables one by one. You may update a single row or multiple rows, depending on your needs.

How to Update a Column

This is perhaps the simplest way of using the UPDATE command. If you'll update a column, you can update either a single row or multiple rows. Here is the syntax for this process:

How to Update Multiple Columns

As stated earlier, you may update many columns using the UPDATE statement. Check this syntax:

This syntax has one SET and three columns: the columns are separated by commas. In general, you should use a comma to segregate different kinds of arguments.

For this example, a comma separates the columns that must be updated.

How to Delete Data

You may use the DELETE statement to eliminate data rows from a table. This statement will remove a whole record (even columns). Thus, you shouldn't use it if you just want to remove some values from several columns. You must be extremely careful when using DELETE – it is an effective and efficient command. In this section, you'll learn about the different techniques in removing data.

To delete a record or multiple records, you should follow this syntax:

This syntax uses WHERE as a supporting clause. This clause is an important aspect of the DELETE command, particularly if you are trying to eliminate specific data rows. Actually, you'll use WHERE with DELETE most of the time. Without the WHERE clause, you'll get a result similar to this one:

Important Note: All data rows inside a table will be deleted if you'll omit WHERE.

Keep in mind that this SQL statement can inflict permanent damages on your database. In ideal situations, you can undo erroneous deletions using a backup file. In some cases, however, it may be impossible to retrieve lost data. If you can no longer recover the deleted data, you have to re-enter it into your database. This is not a problem with a single data row, but this can make you pull your hair if you are dealing with hundreds (or thousands) of data rows.

How to Manage Database Transactions

Simply put, transactions are units or sets of work done on a database. You can accomplish database transactions manually (i.e. by typing) or automatically (i.e. using a database program). For relational databases that use SQL, you can use the DML statements to complete transactions. DML statements were discussed in the previous chapter.

A database transaction can either be a DML command or a sequence of commands. While conducting transactions, all of the transactions need to be successful. If at least one transaction fails, the remaining transactions will fail too.

Here are the characteristics of a database transaction:

- *Each transaction has a starting point and an endpoint.*
- *Each transaction can be undone or saved.*
- *If transactions fail to complete, none of them can be saved.*

Transactional Control

This is the capability to control different transactions that may happen inside a database management system. Whenever you talk about transactions, you will be referring to the DML commands (i.e. UPDATE, DELETE and INSERT).

Once a transaction is successfully completed, you won't see immediate changes in the affected data tables. Sometimes, you have to use transactional control statements to finalize your database transactions. These control statements can help you save or undo the changes you have made.

Here are the control statements that you can use:

- *ROLLBACK*
- *COMMIT*
- *SAVEPOINT*

When a database transaction is completed, the information about it is kept either in an assigned area or a short-term rollback area inside the database. These areas hold transactional information until a control statement is executed. As stated earlier, control statements may save or discard transactions. The rollback area will be emptied once the transaction is saved or discarded.

The image below shows how changes are performed on a database:

The ROLLBACK Statement

You must use this statement to reverse unsaved changes. ROLLBACK can only be applied to transactions made after the last ROLLBACK or COMMIT statement. Here's the syntax for the ROLLBACK statement:

Here, WORK is completely optional.

Important Note: Currently, MySQL doesn't support this statement.

The COMMIT Statement

You'll use this statement to save the changes caused by your transaction. This statement finalizes all transactions completed after the last ROLLBACK or COMMIT statement.

When using this command, you must follow this syntax:

This syntax has a mandatory part: COMMIT. This part comes with a character or statement used to finish the command. The keyword "WORK" is optional: use it to improve the command's user-friendliness.

The SAVEPOINT Statement

This is a part of a transaction where you can undo certain changes without affecting the whole transaction. This is the syntax for SAVEPOINT:

You can only use this statement when creating a SAVEPOINT in transactional commands. If you want to undo changes, you must use ROLLBACK. SAVEPOINT allows you to manage database transactions by dividing them into small groups.

Going Back to a Save Point

If you want to roll back to a certain SAVEPOINT, use the following syntax:

Removing a Save Point

You can use RELEASE SAVEPOINT to remove a save point you have made. After removing a save point this way, you won't be able to use that point in rolling back database changes. You can use the RELEASE SAVEPOINT statement to prevent unwanted reversals of database modifications. Here's the syntax that you should follow:

How to Get Excellent Results from Database Queries

This chapter will focus on database queries. Here, you'll learn how to use the SELECT command on the results of your queries. In general, you will use SELECT lots of times once your database has been established. This command helps you to search and view the information stored in your database.

The Query

Queries are inquiries into a database. These inquiries are submitted through the SELECT command. You must use queries to get data from a database. For example, if you have a product table, you may execute an SQL command to identify your best-selling product. This request for usable product information is normal for modern relational databases.

The Select Command

This command represents the DQL (i.e. Data Query Language) aspect of SQL. You can use the SELECT command to start and execute database queries. In general, this statement cannot stand alone: you have to use additional clauses to make queries possible. Aside from the mandatory clauses, optional clauses exist to help users in improving the effectiveness of database queries.

When using the SELECT command, there are four clauses (also called keywords) that you must consider. These clauses are:

1. SELECT – This command is combined with FROM to obtain data in a readable, organized format. You can use this to determine the data you need to get. Here's the syntax of a basic SELECT command:

The SELECT clause introduces the list of columns you like to see in the search results. FROM, on the other hand, introduces the tables you want to choose data from. You should use the asterisk to indicate that each column will be displayed in the query results. ALL allows you to view all of the values for any column, even redundant data. DISTINCT is an option that you can use to hide duplicate information. As you can see, commas are used to separate the columns for FROM and SELECT.

2. FROM – You should use this clause in combination with SELECT. It's a mandatory element of any database query. The purpose of this clause is to specify the tables that must be accessed during the search. When running a query, you should indicate at least one table in the FROM clause.

The syntax of this clause is:

3. WHERE – This clause can have multiple conditions (i.e. the element of a query that display selective data as selected by the database user). If you are using this feature, you should connect the conditions using the OR and AND operators. This is the syntax for WHERE:

4. ORDER BY – You can use this clause to arrange the output of a database query. This clause organizes the search results using your selected format. By default, this clause organizes query output in an ascending order – the output will be displayed from A-Z if you are working with names. This statement's syntax is:

Case Sensitivity

You should understand this concept completely if you want to use SQL. Usually, SQL statements and clauses are not sensitive to uppercase and lower case characters. That means you can enter clauses and statements with the Caps Lock on: it won't affect your SQL commands in any way.

However, case sensitivity becomes extremely important when you are dealing with data objects. Most of the time, data is stored using uppercase letters. This method helps database users in maintaining the consistency of data.

For example, your database will be inconsistent if you'll enter data this way:

- *JOHN*
- *John*
- *John*

If the data was stored as JOHN and you executed a query for John, you won't get relevant output.

Categorize Information Using Database Operators

Operators – The Basics

Operators are reserved words or characters mainly used in the WHERE clause of SQL statements. As their name suggests, operators are used to perform operations (e.g. comparisons and mathematical operations). Operators can specify parameters for your SQL statements. Lastly, they can connect multiple parameters within the same SQL statement.

This chapter will use the following operators:

- *Logical Operators*
- *Comparison Operators*
- *Arithmetic Operators*
- *Operators for Negating Conditions*

Let's discuss each operator type in detail:

Logical Operators

These operators use keywords to perform comparisons. In this section, you'll learn about the following logical operators:

- *IN*
- *LIKE*
- *UNIQUE*
- *EXISTS*

- *BETWEEN*
- *IS NULL*
- *ANY and ALL*

IN

With this operator, you'll compare a value to a set of specified literal values. You will only get TRUE if at least one of the specified values is equal to the value being tested. Here's an example:

LIKE

Here, you'll use wildcard operators to compare a value against similar ones. You can combine LIKE with the following wildcard operators:

- "_" – (i.e. The underscore)
- "%" – (i.e. The percent sign)

You should use the underscore to represent a character or number. On the other hand, you must use "%" to represent one, zero, or several characters. You may combine these wildcard operators in your SQL statements. Here are some examples:

WHERE PRICE LIKE '100%' - This statement will find values that begin with 100.

WHERE PRICE LIKE '%100%' – This SQL statement will search for values the include 200.

WHERE PRICE LIKE '_11%' – This statement will search for any value that has "11" as its second and third digits.

WHERE PRICE LIKE '1_%_%_%' – This statement will find values that begin with 1 are at least four characters long.

WHERE PRICE LIKE '%1' – This will search for values that have 1 as their last character.

UNIQUE

With this operator, you can check the uniqueness of one or more data rows. Check this simple example:

EXISTS

You can use this operator to find data rows that meet your chosen criteria. Here's an example:

BETWEEN

You can use BETWEEN to find values within a specific range. Here, you'll assign the maximum value and the minimum value. You must include the maximum and minimum values in your conditional set. Check this example:

IS NULL

You can use IS NULL to compare your chosen value with a NULL one. For instance, you can identify the products that don't have wheels by checking for NULL values in the "WHEEL" column of your PRODUCTS_TBL table.

In the example below, you won't get a NULL value:

ANY and ALL

ANY is an operator that can compare a value against any legitimate value in a list. The list of values should have predetermined conditions. Here's an example:

ALL, however, compares your selected value against the values contained in a different value set.

Comparison Operators

These operators can test single values within SQL statements. This category is composed of <, >, <>, and =. You can use these operators to test:

- *Non-equality*
- *Equality*
- *Greater-than values*
- *Less-than values*

Non-equality

As an SQL user, you should use "<>" to test non-equality. The operation gives TRUE if the data is not equal; FALSE if the data is equal.

Important Note: You may also use the "!=" operator. Actually, many SQL implementations are using this operator to test inequality. Check the implementation you are using to find out more about this topic.

Equality

You can use this operator to test single values in your SQL statements. Obviously, "=" (i.e. the equal sign) represents equality. When checking for equality, you will only get data if the chosen values are identical. If the values are equal, you'll get TRUE as the result. If the values aren't equal, you'll get FALSE.

Greater-than, Less-than

In general, "<" and ">" can serve as stand-alone operators. However, you can improve the effectiveness of your operations if you'll combine them with other operators.

Comparison Operators - Simple Combos

You can combine "=" with "<" and ">." Check the examples below:

With "<= 20,000" (i.e. less-than or equal-to 20,000), you'll get 20,000 and all of the values below it. If a database object is within that range, you'll get TRUE from the operation. If the object's value is 20,001 or higher, on the other hand, you will get FALSE.

The second example follows the same principle. The only difference is that you'll get TRUE for objects whose value is 20,000 and above. You'll get FALSE for objects with the value of 19,999 and below.

Arithmetic Operators

These operators can help you perform mathematical operations in the SQL language. In this section, you'll learn about the typical operators used in relational databases: +. -, *, and /.

Let's discuss each operator in detail:

Addition

You can perform addition using "+" (i.e. the plus sign). Study the following SQL statements:

SELECT MATERIALS + OVERHEAD FROM PRODUCTION_COST_TBL – In this SQL statement, you'll add up the values in the MATERIALS column and the OVERHEAD column.

SELECT MATERIALS FROM PRODUCTION_COST_TBL WHERE MATERIALS + OVERHEAD < '500' – This operation will return values where the sum of MATERIALS and OVERHEAD is less than 500.

Subtraction

You can use “-” (i.e. the minus sign) to perform subtraction. To help you understand this process, two examples are given below:

SELECT SALES - COST FROM COMPANY_FINANCIALS_TBL – For this SQL statement, the COST column will be deducted from the SALES column.

SELECT SALES FROM COMPANY_FINANCIALS_TBL WHERE SALES - COST < ‘100000’ – This statement will give you values where SALES minus COST is less than ‘100,000.’

Multiplication

You should use “*” (i.e. the asterisk) to perform multiplication. Check the examples below:

SELECT SALES * 10 FROM COMPANY_FINANCIALS_TBL – The values in the SALES column will be multiplied by ten.

SELECT SALES FROM COMPANY_FINANCIALS_TBL WHERE SALES * 10 < ‘100000’ – This statement will return values where the product of (SALES * 10) is less than 100,000.

Division

You must use "/" (i.e. the slash symbol) when performing division. Here are two examples:

SELECT SALES / 5 FROM COMPANY_FINANCIALS_TBL – The SALES column is divided by 5.

SELECT SALES FROM COMPANY_FINANCIALS_TBL WHERE SALES / 5 < '100000' – This SQL statement will return data rows where the result of (SALES / 5) is less than 100,000.

Some Combinations of Arithmetic Operators

You may combine arithmetic operators to streamline your database processes. Keep in mind that SQL applies the principles of precedence in mathematics. That means you'll perform multiplication and division first. Then, you'll complete the process by performing addition and subtraction. You can only control the sequence of mathematical operations if you will use parentheses.

Important Note: Precedence is the sequence in which mathematical expressions are performed. Here are some basic examples:

EXPRESSION	RESULT
2 + 2 * 5	12
(2 + 2) * 5	20
20 – 8 / 4 + 2	20
(20 – 8) / (4 + 2)	2

When working with multiple arithmetic operators, always apply the principles of precedence. If you'll forget about precedence and the usage of parentheses, you will get inaccurate results from your arithmetic operations in SQL. Logical errors can still exist even if you have perfect syntaxes for your SQL statements.

For the next examples, the parentheses don't influence the result if only division and multiplication are performed. Keep in mind that precedence is not important in these situations. Study these examples:

EXPRESSION	RESULT
8 * 12 / 4	24
(8 * 12) / 4	24
8 * (12/4)	24

Operators for Negating Conditions

In this section, you'll learn how to negate the logical operators discussed above. Negating the effects of logical operators is necessary if you want to alter the viewpoint of a condition.

You should use NOT to cancel the operator it is used for. NOT is a logical operator in SQL that can be utilized with these techniques:

NOT EQUAL

Earlier, you learned how to check for inequality using "<" and ">." It is important to mention inequality here since if you are checking for it, you are already cancelling the "=" operator. Here's another technique that you can use to test inequality:

WHERE PRICE <> ‘’10000’ – Price is not equal to 10,000

WHERE PRICE != ‘10000’ – Price is not equal to 10,000

In the second statement, the "!" negates the comparison for equality. Some SQL implementations allow users to combine "!" with the typical inequality operators (i.e. "<" and ">").

NOT BETWEEN

You can negate BETWEEN using the NOT BETWEEN operator. Here's an example:

WHERE PRICE NOT BETWEEN '5000' AND '10000' – The value of PRICE can't fall within the 5,000 to 10,000 range.

NOT IN

You can use NOT IN to negate the IN operator. In the example below, all prices that are not included in the list will be returned.

WHERE PRICE NOT IN ('200', '300', '400') – Action will only be taken if PRICE is not equal to any value in the list.

NOT LIKE

NOT LIKE negates the wildcard operator LIKE. If you are using NOT LIKE, you will only get values different from the one you specified. Here are some examples:

WHERE PRICE NOT LIKE '100%' – This SQL statement will find values that begin with any number except "100."

WHERE PRICE NOT LIKE '%100%' - This statement will get values that don't have "200" in them.

WHERE PRICE NOT LIKE '_11%' – This SQL statement will give you values that don't have "11" in their second and third positions.

WHERE PRICE NOT LIKE '1_%_%' – This statement WILL NOT find values that begin with 1 and are three characters long.

IS NOT NULL

You can use IS NOT NULL operator to negate IS NULL. This procedure is usually done to check for data that isn't NULL. Here's an example:

WHERE PRICE IS NOT NULL – This operation will return price values that are not null.

NOT EXISTS

This operator can help you negate EXIST. Study the example below:

In this example, the maximum cost is shown in the output section. This is because the cost of all existing records is less than 100.

NOT UNIQUE

Use this operator to negate UNIQUE.

WHERE NOT UNIQUE PRICE (SELECT FROM PRODUCT_TBL) – This statement checks whether there are "non-UNIQUE" prices in the PRODUCT_TBL table.

Conjunctive Operators

Sometimes, you have to use multiple criteria. This is usually the case if you are getting confusing results from your database queries. You can combine different criteria in your SQL statements using the conjunctive operators. These are:

- *OR*
- *AND*

OR

You can use this operator to combine conditions in the WHERE clause of your SQL statement. Before an SQL statement can take any action, the criteria should be TRUE or separated by OR. Here's an example:

WHERE PRICE = '100' OR PRICE = '300' – This statement will find values in the PRICE column that match either 200 or 300.

AND

This operator allows you to include multiple criteria in your SQL statement's WHERE section. Your SQL statement will only take action if the criteria segregated by AND are all TRUE. Analyze the example below:

WHERE PRODUCT_ID = 'ABC' AND PRICE = '200' – This statement will look for data objects whose PRODUCT_ID value is ABC and PRICE value is 200.

Important Note: Keep in mind that you can always combine multiple operators and conditions in your SQL statements. You can also improve the readability of your statements by using parentheses.

4. Database Administration

Once you have your database up and running with tables and queries, it is up to you to keep the production database running smoothly. The database will need regular checks to ensure that it continues to perform as originally intended. If a database is poorly maintained, it can easily result in a connected website performing poorly, or it could result in down time or even data loss. There is usually a person, known as a Database Administrator or DBA, designated to look after the database. However, it is usually someone who is not a DBA who needs help with the database.

There are a number of different tasks that you can perform when carrying out maintenance, including the following:

- Database Integrity: When you check the integrity of the database, you are running checks on the data to make sure that both the physical and logical structure of the database is consistent and accurate.
- Index Reorganization: Once you start to insert and delete data on your database, there is going to be

fragmentation (or a scattering) of indexes. Reorganizing the index will bring everything back together again and increase speed.

- Rebuild Index: You don't have to perform an index reorganization; you can drop an index and then recreate it.
- Database Backup: One of the most important tasks to perform. There are a number of different ways in which you can back up the database. These include: full - backs up the database entirely, differential - backs up the database since the last full backup, and transaction log - only backs up the transaction log.
- Check Database Statistics: You can check the statistics of the database that are kept on queries. If you update the statistics, which can get out of date, you can help aid the queries that are being run.
- Data and Log File: In general, make sure the data and log files are kept separate from each other. These files will grow when your database is being used, and it's best to allocate them an appropriate size going forward (and not just enable them to grow).

Depending on your database, some tasks may be more useful than others. Apart from database backup, which is probably mandatory if it's in production, you can pick through the other tasks depending on the state of the database.

For example, should the fragmentation of the database be below 30%, then you can choose to perform an index reorganization. However, if the database fragmentation is greater than 30%, then you should rebuild the index. You can rebuild the index on a weekly basis or more often, if possible.

You can run a maintenance plan on the SQL Server via its Server Agent depending on database requirements. It's important to set the times appropriately, not when your application is expected to be busy. You can choose a time, or you can run it when the server CPU is not busy. Choosing to run when the server is not busy is a preferred option for larger databases rather than selecting a particular time, as there may be no guaranteed time when the CPU will be idle. However, it is usually only a concern if your application is quite big and has a lot of requests.

When you do rebuild the indexes, it is important that you have the results sorted in tempdb. When using tempdb, the old indexes are kept until new ones are added. Normally, rebuilding the indexes uses the fixed space that was allocated to the database. Therefore, if you run out of disk space, then you would not be able to complete the index rebuilding. It's possible to use the tempdb and not have to increase the database disk size. The database maintenance can be run either synchronously (at the same time) or asynchronously (once task has been completed). However, you should ensure the tasks are running in the right order.

Setting up a Maintenance Plan in SQL Server

To set up a maintenance plan in SQL Server, you must first get the server to show advanced options. This is achieved through executing the following code in SQL Server as a new query:

```
sp_configure 'show advanced options', 1

GO

RECONFIGURE

GO
```

```
sp_configure 'Agent XPs', 1
GO
RECONFIGURE
GO
```

The SQL Server will now display the advanced options. Left-click the + icon to the left of Management, which is on the left-hand side of SQL Server Management Studio. Now, left-click Maintenance Plans and then right-click Maintenance Plans. Select New Maintenance Plan Wizard.

Enter an appropriate maintenance plan name and description. From here, you can either run one or all tasks in one plan and have as many plans as you want. After you have assigned a name, choose Single Schedule and click Next.

You will see a number of options that you can pick for your maintenance, including:

- Checking your Database Integrity
- Shrinking the Database

- Reorganizing Index
- Rebuilding the Index
- Updating the Statistics
- Clean up History
- Executing SQL Server Agent Job
- Back Up – full, differential or transaction log
- Maintenance Cleanup Task

Select which you want to perform (in this example, select all). This wizard will bring you through each of the items you have selected to fine-tune them.

Once you select the items you want in your plan, click Next. You can now rearrange them in the order that you want them to complete. It's best to have Database Backup first in case of power failure, so select it and move it to the top of the list. Click Next.

Define Backup Database (Full) Task

This screen will give you the freedom to pick which full database backup you wish to perform on. The best practice is to keep one plan per database; select one database and select Next.

Define Database Check Integrity Task

The integrity task is an SQL Server command that aims at inspecting the database's integrity to make sure that everything is stable. Select a database and click Next.

Define Shrink Database Task

You can now configure to shrink the database in order to free up space in the next screen. This will only shrink space if available, but should you need space in the future, you will have to allocate it again. However, this step will help backup speeds. Most developers don't use this feature that much. Click Next after selecting a database to shrink.

Define Reorganize Index Task

The next screen is the Define Reorganize Index Task screen. When you add, modify, and delete indexes you will, like tables, need to reorganize them. The process is the same as a hard disk, where you have fragmented files and space scattered across the disk. Perform this task once per week for a busy database. You can choose to compact large object, which compacts any index that has large binary object data. Click Next to proceed to the next screen.

Define Rebuild Index Task

This screen covers individual index rows and involves either reorganizing or reindexing. Doing both together in one plan is pointless. Depending on your fragmentation level, pick one or the other. In this example, select your database and sort results in tempdb. Click Next to proceed.

Define Update Statistics Task

The update statistics task helps the developer keep track of data retrieval as its created, modified, and deleted. You can keep the statistics up-to-date by performing this plan. Statistics for both indexes and individual columns are kept. Select your database and click Next to proceed.

Define History Cleanup Task

You should now see this screen, which specifies the historical data to delete. You can specify a shorter time frame to keep the backup and recovery, agent job history, and maintenance place on the drop down. Click Next to proceed.

Define Backup Database (Differential) Task

This screen allows you to back up every page in the database that has been altered since the previous or last full backup. Select a database you wish to use and click Next.

Define Backup Database (Transaction Log) Task

The transaction log backup backs up all the log records since the last backup. You can choose a folder to store it in. Performing this type of backup is the least resource-intensive backup. Select a database and storage location and click Next.

Define Execute SQL Server Agent Job Task

The SQL Server Agent Job Task deals with jobs that are outside the wizard. For example, it can check for nulls, check whether the database meets specified standards, and more. Any jobs that are specified in SQL Server Agent Job Task are listed here. Click Next to proceed.

Define Maintenance Cleanup Task

This screen defines the cleanup action of the maintenance task. This ensures that files are not taking up unnecessary space, and you can specify where to store them. You can also delete specific backup files. Click Next to proceed.

Report Options

The next screen covers where you want to store the report of the maintenance plan. Make a note of where you are going to store it. You need to have email setup on SQL Server in order to email it. Click Next to proceed.

Complete the Wizard

The final screen is a complete review of the wizard. You can review the summary of the plan and which options were selected. Clicking Finish ends the wizard and creates the plan. You should now see a success screen with the completed tasks.

Running the Maintenance Plan

Once you successfully complete the maintenance wizard, the next step is to run the plan you created. In order to get the plan to run, you need to have the SQL Server Agent running. It is visible two below Management on SQL Server Management Studio. You can left-click SQL Server Agent, then right-click and select Start.

Alternatively, you can press the Windows key and press the letter R, then type services.msc and hit Enter. Once Services appears, scroll down and look for the SQL Server Agent (MSSQLEXPRESS). This book instructed you to install SQL Server Express, but you can select the other versions like (MSSQLSERVER) if you installed that. Left-click it, then right-click it and select Start.

You can go back to SSMS and right-click on the maintenance plan you created under maintenance plans, then select Execute. This will now run your plan. Upon successful completion of the plan, click OK and close the dialogue box. You can view the reports by right-clicking the maintenance plan you created and selecting View History. On the left-hand side are all the different plans in SQL Server, while the results of the specific plan are on the right.

Emailing the Reports

A lot of DBAs like to get their database reports via email. What you need to do is set up a database mail before you can fire off emails, and then set up a Server agent to send the emails.

Configuring the Database Mail

The first step is to right-click Database mail in SSMS and select Configure Database Mail. A wizard screen will appear; click Next. Now select, the first choice–Set Up Database Mail–and click Next. Enter a profile name and, if you want, an optional description of the profile. Now, click on the Add button to the right.

This will bring you to an add New Database Mail Account – SMTP. You need to enter the SMTP details for an email account. You may want to set up a new email account for this service. You can search online for SMTP details, and Gmail works quite well (server name: smtp.gmail.com, port number 587, SSL required, tick basic authentication, and confirm password). Click on OK. Click Next, and select Public; it is important to do this so it can be used by the rest of the database. Set it as Default Profile, click Next, and click Next again. You should now get a success screen. Click Close.

SQL Server Agent

To send off the database email, you need to set up a Server Agent. Start by right-clicking on SQL Server Agent → New → Operator. Give the operator a name like Maintenance Plan Operator, enter in the email address to which you want the report delivered, and click OK.

Now, right-click the maintenance plan that you have successfully executed and select Modify. The maintenance plan design screen will appear on the right-hand side, where you can see some graphics of the tasks completed in it. Now, click on Reporting and Logging; it is an icon situated on the menu bar of the design plan, to the left of Manage Connections.

The Reporting and Logging window will appear. Choose the option to Send Report to an Email Recipient, and select the maintenance plan operator you just created. The next time you run the plan, an email will be sent to the email address.

The running and maintenance of a database is an important job. Having the right plan for your database will ensure that it continues to work as originally designed, and you will be able to quickly identify and fix database errors or slowdowns early on.

Backup and Recovery

The most important task a DBA can perform is backing up the essential database in use. When you create a maintenance plan, it's important to have backup and recovery at the top of the maintenance list in case the job doesn't get fully completed. Firstly, it is important to understand the transaction log and why it is important.

The Transaction Log

Whenever a change is made to the database, be it a transaction or modification, it is stored in the transaction log. The transaction log is the most important file in an SQL Server database, and everything revolves around either saving it or using it.

Every transaction log can facilitate transaction recovery, recover all incomplete transactions, roll forward a restored file, filegroup, or page to a point of failure, replicate transactions, and facilitate disaster recovery.

Recovery

The first step in backing up a database is choosing a recovery option for the database. You can perform the three types of backups when the SQL Server is online, and even while users are making requests from the database at the same time.

When you perform the process of doing backup and restore in the SQL Server, you do so within the confines of the recovery model designed to control the maintenance of the transactional log. Such a recovery model is known to be a database property aimed at ensuring that all transactions are logged in a certain procedure.

There are three different recovery options: simple, full, and bulk-logged.

Simple Recovery

You cannot backup the transaction log when utilizing the simple recovery model. Usually, this model is used when updates are infrequent. Transactions are minimally logged and the log will be truncated.

Full Recovery

In the full recovery model, the transaction log backup must be taken. Only when the backup process begins will the transaction log be truncated. You can recover to any point in time. However, you also need the full chain of log files to restore the database to the nearest time possible.

Bulk-Logged Recovery

This model is designed to be utilized for short-term use when you use a bulk import operation. You use it along with the full recovery model whenever you don't need a recovery to a certain point in time. It has performance gains and doesn't fill up the transaction log.

Changing the Recovery Model

To change the recovery model, you can right-click on a database in SQL Server Management Studio and select Properties. Then, select Options and choose the recovery model from the drop-down box. Alternatively, you can use one of the following:

- ALTER DATABASE SQLEbook SET RECOVERY SIMPLE

GO

- ALTER DATABASE SQLEbook SET RECOVERY FULL

GO

- ALTER DATABASE SQLEbook SET RECOVERY BULK_LOGGED

GO

Backups

There are three types of backup: full, differential, and transaction log. When Database Administrators set up a backup plan, they base their plan on two measures: Recovery Time Objective (RTO) and Recovery Point Objective (RPO). The RTO records the period to recover after a notification of a disruption in the business process. RPO measures the timeframe that might pass during a disruption before the data size that has been lost exceeds the maximum limit of the business process.

If there was an RPO of only 60 minutes, you couldn't achieve this goal if your backup was set to every 24 hours. You need to set your backup plan based on these two measures.

Full Backup

When you create a full backup, the SQL Server creates a CHECKPOINT which ensures that any exiting dirty pages are written to disk. Then, the SQL Server backs up each and every page on the database. It then backs up the majority of the transaction log to ensure there is transactional consistency. What all of this means is that you are able to restore your database to the most recent point and recover all the transactions, including those right up to the very beginning of the backup.

Exercising this alone is the least flexible option. Essentially, you are only able to restore your database back to one point of time, which the is the last full backup. Thus, if the database went corrupt two hours from midnight (and your backup is at midnight) your RPO would be 22 hours. In addition, if a user truncated a table two hours from midnight, you would have the same 22-hour loss of business transactions.

Transaction Log Backup

With the transaction log backup, the SQL Server backs up the data in the transaction log only, in other words, only the transactions that were recently committed to the database. The transaction log is not as resource-hungry and is considered important because it can perform backups more often without having an impact on database performance.

If you select Full Recovery mode, you can run both a full backup and a transaction log backup. You can also run more frequent backups since running the transaction log backup takes less resources. This is a very good choice if your database is updated throughout the day.

In scheduling transaction log backups, it's best to follow the RPO. For example, if there is an RPO of 60 minutes, then set the log file backups to 60 minutes. However, you must check the RTO for such a backup. If you had an RPO of 60 minutes and are only performing a full backup once a week, you might not be able to restore all 330 backups in the allotted time.

Differential Backup

To get around the problem mentioned above, you can add differential backups to the plan. A differential backup is cumulative, which mean a serious reduction in the number of backups you would need to recover your database to the point just before failure.

The differential backup, as its name suggests, backs up every page in the database that has since been modified since the last backup. The SQL Server keeps track of all the different pages that have been modified via flags and DIFF pages.

Performing a Backup

To back up a database, right-click the database in SSMS, then select Tasks → Backup. You can select what kind of backup to perform (full, differential, or transaction log) and when to perform the backup. The copy-only backup allows you to perform a backup that doesn't affect the restore sequence.

Restoring a Database

When you want to restore a database in SSMS, right-click the database, then select Tasks → Restore → Database. You can choose the database contained in the drop-down menu and keep the rest of the tabs populated.

If you click on Timeline, you can see a graphical diagram of when the last backup was created, which shows how much data was lost. You may have the option of recovering up to the end of a log, or a specific date and time.

The Verify Backup Timeline media button enables you to verify the backup media before you actually restore it. If you want to change where you are going to store the backup, you can click on Files to select a different location. You can specify the restore options that you want to use on the Options page. Either overwrite the existing database or keep it. The recovery state either brings the database online or allows further backups to be applied.

Once you click OK, the database will be restored.

Attaching and Detaching Databases

The method of attaching and detaching databases is similar to that of backups and restores.

Essentially, here are the details of this method:

- Allows you to copy the .MDF file and .LDF file to a new disk or server.
- Performs like a backup and restore process, but can be faster at times, depending on the situation.
- The database is taken offline and cannot be accessed by any users or applications. It will remain offline until it's been reattached.

So, which one should you choose? Though a backup is the ideal option, there are cases where an attachment/detachment of the database may be your only choice.

Consider the following scenario:

Your database contains many filegroups. Attaching those can be quite cumbersome.

The appropriate solution is to back up the database and then restore it to the desired destination, as it will group all of the files together in the backup process.

Based on the size of the database, the backup/restore process takes a long time. However, the attaching/detaching of the database could be much quicker if it's needed as soon as possible.

In this scenario, you can take the database offline, detach it, and re-attach it to the new destination.

As mentioned above, there are two main file groups when following the method of attaching databases. These files are .MDF and .LDF. The .MDF file is the database's primary data file, which holds its structure and data. The .LDF file holds the transactional logging activity and history.

However, a .BAK file that's created when backing up a database, groups all of the files together and you restore different file versions from a single backup set.

Consider your situation before taking either option, but also consider a backup and restore first before looking into the attach/detach method as your next option. Also, be sure to test it before you move forward with live data!

Attaching/Detaching the AdventureWorks2012 Database

Since you already attached this database, we'll have you detach it from the server. After that, you'll attach it again using SQL syntax.

Detaching the Database

In SQL Server, there's a stored procedure that will detach the database for you. This particular stored procedure resides in the "master" database. Under the hood, you can see the complexity of the stored procedure by doing the following:

1. Click to expand the Databases folder

2. Click on System Databases, then the "master" database

3. Click on Programmability

4. Click on Stored Procedures, then System Stored Procedures

5. Find sys.sp_detach_db, right-click it and select 'Modify' in SSMS to see its syntax

For this, you'll just execute the stored procedure as is.

Below is the syntax:

```
USE master

GO

ALTER DATABASE DatabaseName SET SINGLE_USER
WITH ROLLBACK IMMEDIATE
GO

EXEC master.dbo.sp_detach_db @dbname =
N'DatabaseName',
@skipchecks = 'false'
GO
```

We'll expand a little on what is happening. You want to use the "master" database to alter the database you'll be detaching and set it to single user instead of multi-user.

Last, the value after @dbname allows you to specify the name of the database to be detached, and the @skipchecks set to false means that the database engine will update the statistics information, identifying that the database has been detached. It's ideal to set this as @false whenever detaching a database so that the system holds current information about all databases.

Attaching Databases

Once you have detached your database, if you navigate to where your data directory is, you'll see that the AdventureWorks2012_Data.MDF file still exists – which it should since you only detached it and didn't delete it.

Next, take the file path of the .MDF file and copy and paste it in some place that you can easily access, like notepad. The location we use is C:\Program Files\Microsoft SQL Server\MSSQL13.MSSQLSERVER\MSSQL\DATA.

Now, go back into SSMS and click on the New Query button (if you're already connected). If you have not connected, then go ahead and connect to your instance.

Once you've connected to your instance and opened up a new query session, you'll just need to use the path of where the data file is stored. Once you have that, you can enter that value in the following SQL syntax examples in order to attach your database.

Below is the syntax for attaching database files and log files. Though in the following exercise, you'll be skipping attaching the log file completely, since you're not attaching this to a new server. Therefore, you may omit the statement to attach the log file.

```
CREATE DATABASE DatabaseName ON
(FILENAME = 'C:\SQL Data Files\DatabaseName.mdf'),
(FILENAME = 'C:\SQL Data
Files\DatabaseName_log.ldf') FOR ATTACH
```

In the above example, we are calling out the statement to attach the log file if one is available. However, if you happen to not have the .LDF file and only the .MDF file, then that's fine, too. You can just attach the .MDF file and the database engine will create a new log file and start writing activity to that particular log.

5. Performing CRUD Operations

Now is time to perform CRUD operations on the database. CRUD is abbreviation of Create, Read, Update and Delete. These are the four most fundamental database operations. In this chapter we will see how to perform these operations.

Creating Data

To create data inside a table the INSERT query is used. The syntax for insert query is as follows:

INSERT INTO TABLE (Column1, Column2, Column3 .... Column N)

VALUES (Value1, Value2, Value3 .... Value N),

(Value1, Value2, Value3 .... Value N),

(Value1, Value2, Value3 .... Value N)

The syntax for insert query is simple; you have to use keywords INSERT INTO TABLE followed by a pair of parenthesis. Inside the parenthesis you have to specify comma separated list of the columns where you want to insert the data. Next VALUES keyword is used followed by a pair of parenthesis that contain comma separated list of values that are to be stored in the columns. You can store multiple records at once. Each set of columns should be separated by others via commas. It is important to mention that sequence of columns and values should be similar.

If you do not specify the columns within the parenthesis after the INSERT INTO TABLE keywords, the default table scheme is used.

Let's insert some data into our Hospital database. As with the table creation, first you should insert the records to the tables that do not have any foreign key. We will start with the Patients table. Take a look at the following query:

USE Hospital;

INSERT INTO Patients
VALUES ('Tom', 20, 'Male' ,'O+', 123589746),
('Kimer', 45,'Female', 'AB+', 45686412),
('James', 16,'Male', 'O-', 78452369),
('Matty', 43,'Female', 'B+', 15789634),
('Sal', 24,'Male', 'O+', 48963214),

```
('Julie', 26,'Female', 'A+', 12478963),
('Frank', 35,'Male', 'A-', 85473216),
('Alex', 21,'Male', 'AB-', 46971235),
('Hales', 54,'Male', 'B+', 74698125),
('Elice', 32,'Female', 'O+', 34169872)
```

In the above query we inserted records of 10 random patients in the Patients table. Here we did not specify the column names; therefore the default column sequence will be used. The values are inserted according to the default column sequence. By default, id is the first column of the Patients. However it has Identity constraint, therefore we do not need to add any value for the id. It will be automatically added. The second column is the name column. The first value will be inserted in this column. Be careful, the name column only accepts string type data. So you must insert string. To create string, enclose the value inside single quotes. Similar, age is the second column of the Patients table and it is of integer data type therefore we enter number as second value in our insert statement.

In the same way, let's insert data into Examinations and Doctors table. The following query inserts data in the Examinations table.

```
USE Hospital;

INSERT INTO Examinations
VALUES('XRay', 750),
('Ultrasound', 600),
('LFT', 800),
('RFT', 900),
 ('HIV', 500)
```

Similarly, let's insert some records in the Doctor's table.

```
USE Hospital;

INSERT INTO Doctors
VALUES('Orland', 'MS', 'Nephrology'),
('Mark', 'HOD', 'Pathology'),
('Evens', 'Professor', 'Cardiology'),
('John','Demonstrator', 'Pediatrician'),
 ('Fred', 'DMS', 'Neurology')
```

We have added data to all the independent tables, now let's some data to the Patient_Visits table. It has a foreign key columpatient id. This column references the id column of the Patients table. This means that patient_id column of Patient_Visits table can only have values that exist in the id column of the Patients table.

In Patients table, the id column has values between 1-10. We will randomly insert these values in the patient_id column. The following script inserts some random records in Patient_Visits table.

```
USE Hospital;

INSERT INTO Patient_Visits
VALUES(1, '19-Apr-2012'),
(2, '19-May-2012'),
(4, '25-Feb-2013'),
(6, '30-Nov-2014'),
(2, '21-Sep-2015'),
(3, '10-Oct-2011'),
(7, '01-Jan-2010'),
(9, '25-May-2012'),
(4, '17-Nov-2012'),
(8, '08-Sep-2016'),
(3, '19-Jan-2013'),
(10, '20-May-2011'),
(3, '17-Feb-2012'),
(7, '19-Mar-2014'),
(10, '05-May-2015'),
(8, '14-Feb-2011'),
(6, '29-Nov-2016'),
```

(10, '18-May-2010'),
(9, '09-Jun-2015'),
(8, '08-Sep-2014')

Now let's insert dummy records to the Treatments and Patient_Examinations table. Treatments table has two foreign key columns patient_id and doctor_id. The former references the id column of Patients table and while the latter references the id column of the Doctors table. So while inserting records for these foreign key columns we should insert only those values that exist in the corresponding referenced columns. The following script inserts record in the Treatment table.

USE Hospital;

INSERT INTO Treatment
VALUES (1,3, 'Fit'),
(1,3, 'Good condition'),
(2,5, 'Needs more treatment'),
(1,4, 'Referred for XRay'),
(8,1, 'Medicnes recommended'),
(5,2, 'Fit'),
(9,3, 'Perfect')

In the same way, execute the following script to add data to Patient_Examination table

```
USE Hospital

INSERT INTO Patient_Examination
VALUES (1,3, 'Positive'),
(1,3, 'Negative'),
(2,5, 'Positive'),
(1,4, 'Negative'),
(8,1, 'Positive'),
(5,2, 'Negative'),
 (9,3, 'Positive')
```

Selecting Data

We have inserted data in all of our tables. Now is the time to retrieve that data. To do in SQL, we use SELECT query. You can either select data from all the columns or data from individual columns. The syntax for both operations is as follows:

Selecting all columns

```
SELECT * FROM Table_Name
```

Selecting Individual Columns

SELECT column1, column2, column3 ... columnN FROM Table_Name

Let's select all the records from the Patients table. Execute following query:

SELECT * FROM Patients

This query will retrieve all records with all column values from Patients table. The result of the above query will look like this:

id	name	age	gender	blood_group	phone
1	Tom	20	Male	O+	123589746
2	Kimer	45	Female	AB+	45686412
3	James	16	Male	O-	78452369
4	Matty	43	Female	B+	15789634
5	Sal	24	Male	O+	48963214
6	Julie	26	Female	A+	12478963
7	Frank	35	Male	A-	85473216

8	Alex	21	Male	AB-	46971235
9	Hales	54	Male	B+	74698125
10	Elice	32	Female	O+	34169872

For instance if you want to retrieve only the name, and blood_group columns for all the records in the Patients table, you can execute following query.

SELECT name, blood_group FROM Patients

The result set will look like this:

name	blood_group
Tom	O+
Kimer	AB+
James	O-
Matty	B+
Sal	O+
Julie	A+
Frank	A-

Alex	AB-
Hales	B+
Elice	O+

Updating Data

To update existing table data, the UPDATE query is used. The syntax of the update query looks like this:

```
UPDATE Table_Name

 SET Column_Name = Value
```

Let's increase the price of all the examinations by 10%. To do so we have to update the value of the price column of the Examinations table by multiplying it with 1.1. The following update query performs this operation.

```
UPDATE Examinations

 SET price = price * 1.1
```

Deleting Data

DELETE query is used to delete records from a table. The syntax of DELETE query is as follows:

```
DELETE FROM Table_Name
```

To delete all the records from Patient_Visits table, execute following query. (Do not forget to reinsert records in the Patient_Visits table. We will use this data to perform queries in the upcoming chapter)

```
DELETE FROM Patient_Visits
```

In this chapter we learned to create, insert, update and delete table records. However we saw that these operations are being performed on all the records. What if we want to delete only specific records? For instance what we will do if want to update records of only female patients?

6. The Hard Hitting Concept Of Nested Queries And Recursive

Just as the title suggests, in this chapter we are going to be dealing with two very distinct yet crucial aspects of SQL programming. Let's start by talking about Subqueries first which will basically be covering the Nested Queries part.

What Exactly Are Nested Queries!

We have already discussed in details about the WHERE clause, Nested queries are basically the enclosing statements within the WHERE clause that defines what function the WHERE clause is going to perform.

NESTED Queries For Returning Multiple Rows

We will be elaborating this whole concept through the usage of a simple example. Let us consider for a moment that you are working for a world renowned company which specializes in assembling various components and bringing them together for you to conveniently purchase them. The whole structure of your company might be comprised of many tables, but you are only concerned with COMPONENT, PRODUCT and COMP_USED tables as illustrated below.

Product

Column	Type	Constraints
Model	CHAR (6)	PRIMARY KEY
ProdName	CHAR (35)	
ProdDesc	CHAR (31)	
ListPrice	NUMERIC (9,2)	

Component

Column	Type	Constraints
CompID	CHAR (6)	PRIMARY KEY
CompType	CHAR (10)	
CompDesc	CHAR (31)	

COMP_USED

Column	Type	Constraints
Model	CHAR (6)	FOREIGN KEY (for PRODUCT)
CompID	CHAR (6)	FOREIGN KEY (for COMPONENT)

The skeleton which you will be using here to acquire the information you desire is the formation of Subqueries with the usage of IN keyword.

```
SELECT column_list
        FROM table
        HERE expression IN (subquery) ;
```

The above syntax implies that the "WHERE" clause is going to be bringing out the information that is present inside the list to which the expression is pointing towards.

From the above example, if we want to bring out all the monitors from our company, we can write a code similar to:

```
SELECT Model
            FROM COMP_USED
            WHERE CompID IN
                        (SELECT CompID
                                    FROM COMPONENT
                                        WHERE   CompType   =
'Monitor');
```

What this code will do is to return all the CompID for every present row where the CompType matches with "Monitor"

The opposite of the IN syntax is the NOT IN syntax which will bring out the information that does not contain the specified field. Following through our given example, if we wanted to bring out a list of all the products that did not fall under as MONITOR, the following code would've been used

```
SELECT Model
        FROM COMP_USED
        WHERE CompID NOT IN
                (SELECT CompID
                        FROM COMPONENT
                        WHERE CompType =
'Monitor')) ;
```

Just as a head up, we would also like you to familiarize yourself with the DISTINCT keyword.

Using this keyword, you will be able to eliminate all the duplicate rows (if any) from your result with ease. The following example shows how that should be done:

```
SELECT DISTINC Model
        FROM COMP_USED
        WHERE CompID NOT IN
```

```
(SELECT CompID
        FROM COMPONENT
            WHERE CompType = 'Monitor'));
```

Introducing The All, Any and Some Quantifiers

Here you will need to use a combination of ALL, SOME or ANY quantifier with comparison operators in order to make sure that the final result is single value form.

Let us consider the table below:

SELECT * FROM NATIONAL

First Name	Last Name	Complete Games
Sal	Maglie	11
Don	Newcombe	9
Sandy	Koufax	13
Don	Drysdale	12

Bob	Turley	8

SELECT * FROM AMERICAN

First Name	Last Name	Complete Games
Whitey	Ford	12
Don	Larson	10
Bob	Turley	8
Allie	Reynolds	14

Here we are going to making an assumption that we need all the information of pitchers who have completed the most game and are from American League. The code for the said example would be:

```
SELECT *

        FROM AMERICAN

        WHERE CompleteGames > ALL
```

(SELECT CompleteGames FROM NATIONAL) ;

This should bear the result similar to:

FirstName	LastName	CompleteGames
----------	---------	---------
Allie	Reynolds	14

The Insertion Of Subqueries With UPDATE, INSERT and DELETE Statements

As you may already notice, subqueries are very versatile when it comes to being able to combine with different statements in order to manipulate multiple data. Combining the WHERE clause (with Subqueries) alongside any of the UPDATE, INSERT or DELETE statement you will also be able to obtain some pretty interesting results.

Continuing from the example of our hypothetical company, if at one point, we want to increase our credit for all last month purchases by 10%, would update our data as follows:

```
UPDATE TRANSMASTER
        SET NetAmount = NetAmount * 0.9
        WHERE SaleDate > (CurrentDate - 30) DAY
AND CustID =
              (SELECT CustID
                    FROM CUSTOMER
                      WHERE Company =
'Olympic Sales') ;
```

Dealing With The Concept Of Recursion

Now that we are done with the first part of this chapter, let us talk about Recursion. So, this is primarily a feature which has been around for quiet sometime in other languages. But it took an unfortunate delay to be integrated with the SQL framework. To understand recursion, you will need to understand a simple mechanism.

In any programming language such as LISP, Logo, C++ or SQL, whenever you are defining a function which will perform a specific action, the program automatically imitates that function by creating a command called "function call". A simplest example of recursion taking place would be a scenario where, alongside while performing a function, the function starts by calling itself!

To make things more clear, let us show you an example of recursion through a program written in C++ that has been designed to draw a spiral on your monitor. Keep in mind that it has been assumed that the drawing tool is initially pointing towards the top of the screen.

The code for the program is

```
void spiral(int segment)

        line(segment)

        left_turn(90)

        spiral(segment + 1)

} ;
```

When you are going to start the program by calling spiral (1) the following actions are going to take place

- Spiral(1) draws just a one unit line alongside the top of the screen

- Spiral(1) takes a 90 degree turn to the left
- Spiral(1) calls upon spiral(2)
- Spiral(2) draws just a one unit line alongside the top of the screen
- Spiral(2) takes a 90 degree turn to the left

And so on the cycle continues, until eventually you will end up with this.

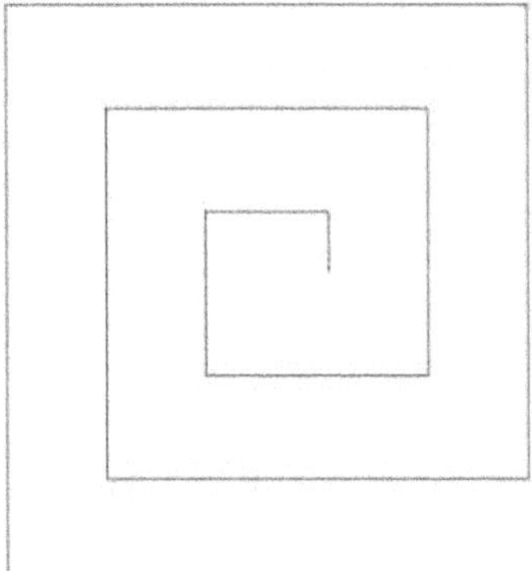

Notice how the program is calling upon itself over and over again? That is recursion. You can relate them to simple loops as found in Java.

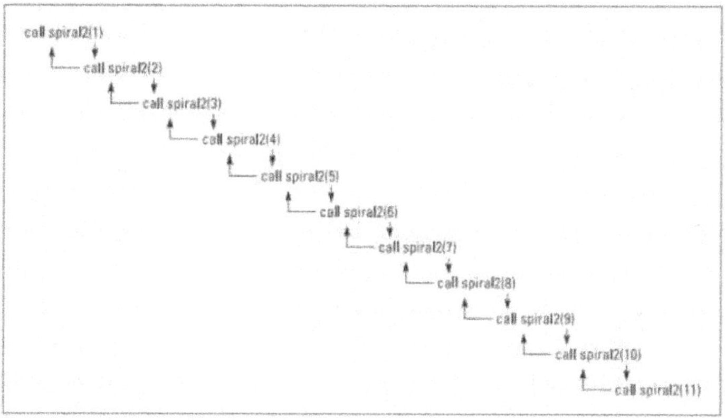

call spiral2(1)
call spiral2(2)
call spiral2(3)
call spiral2(4)
call spiral2(5)
call spiral2(6)
call spiral2(7)
call spiral2(8)
call spiral2(9)
call spiral2(10)
call spiral2(11)

The Introduction To Recursive Query

Now that you know what recursion is, it should not be difficult for you to grasp the concept of a recursive query. This is simply a query which is functionally dependent upon itself. So, for example if we have an expression embodied within query 1, running that very expression would invoke itself in the body of the query expression.

Sounds weird? Don't worry! Let us clear things up with a real life example.

Let's consider in a scenario that a hypothetical Airlines called "The Secretive International" has decided to give you a completely free air travel opportunity. The obvious question that will pop up in your mind then is "Where can I go for free?"

Below is a table which contains the flight number, source and destination of the available flights

Using the data above, you will want to create a complete table which will act as your vacation planner using the code below.

```
CREATE                    TABLE                    LI
GHT (

          FlightNo            INTEGER
    NOT NULL,

          Source            CHAR (30),

          Destination CHAR (30) );
```

Once you have chosen a starting destination, you are going to want to decide which cities you will be able to reach. If say for example, you are starting from Portland or from Montgomery! Finding a solution to such a query can be outright cumbersome if you tackle each of the following queries one by one. This is a perfect example where recursive query should be utilized through the code below:

```
WITH RECURSIVE
        REACHABLEFROM (Source, Destination)
            AS (SELECT Source, Destination
                    FROM FLIGHT
            UNION
            SELECT in.Source, out.Destination
                    FROM REACHABLEFROM in,
FLIGHT out
                    WHERE in.Destination =
out.Source
            )
        SELECT * FROM REACHABLEFROM
        WHERE Source = 'Portland';
```

The result will be something similar to the table below which shows you through recursion, the possible reachable cities when starting from each of the source cities.

7. Making Your Database Secure

Being a system administrator for large scale databases is not easy as you may think. Not only are you going to deal with the demands of the clients, but you will also have to maintain and provide a much secured environment so that your clients can feel safe knowing that their data is in safe hands. SQL provides a diverse array of functions which can be combined to create very sophisticated and seamless security systems that will give you control over granting or revoking access rights to individual users.

The 9 Functions of Control

The following functions contribute to the way you can re-enforce your security system.

- INSERT
- DELETE
- UPDATE
- SELECT
- REFRENCE
- USAGE

- UNDER
- TRIGGER
- EXECUTE

The Hierarchy Of Database System

When it comes to establishing a secured system, it is crucial that you understand the hierarchy of the database system. The hierarchy gives you an idea of how the whole system is working. At its very core, the parts of the SQL security system have been classified as follows:

- *The DBA (Database Administrator):* The database administrator is generally the person who holds the supreme authority over all the actions occurring within a database. All the powers of modification are at the disposal of DBA and he can very well destroy everything with just a single mistake.
- *Database Object Owners:* This is another set of user with high privileges. In general, the people who create any data objects such as tables, views etc. are referred to as being the owners of those objects and they have privileges within

them associated with the manipulations and protection of those objects.

- *The Public:* Once the DBA and Database Owners have been taken out, the remaining people working with the database with no special privilege are called the PUBLIC. The access rights of the public largely relies on the rights granted to them from the privileged users.
-

Setting the Privileges

As the DBA of a database, you will have the power to allow certain users access specific parts of your database and prevent them from accessing the rest. This is done using the GRANT statement.

```
GRANT privilege-list

        ON object

        TO user-list

        [WITH HIERARCHY OPTION]

        [WITH GRANT OPTION]

        [GRANTED BY grantor] ;
```

A Privilege here is defined as

SELECT

| DELETE

| INSERT [(column-name [, column-name]...)]

| UPDATE [(column-name [, column-name]...)]

| REFERENCES [(column-name [, column-name]...)]

| USAGE

| UNDER

| TRIGGER

| EXECUTE

While an object is defined as

[TABLE] <table name>

| DOMAIN <domain name>

| COLLATION <collation name>

| CHARACTER SET <character set name>

| TRANSLATION <transliteration name>

| TYPE <schema-resolved user-defined type name>

| SEQUENCE <sequence generator name>

| <specific routine designator>

And finally the user list is as follows

login-ID [, login-ID]...

| PUBLIC

The Significance Of Role Assignment

Roles are nothing but an alternative to user name which can be used as an authorization identifier. You can set a role using a syntax such as

CREATE ROLE SalesClerk ;

After which, you can assign people to the created role using GRANT

GRANT SalesClerk to Becky ;

This essentially will help you create a group of people with similar privileges with ease.

A role can be allowed to INSERT data by:

```
GRANT INSERT
        ON CUSTOMER
        TO SalesClerk ;
```

A role can be allowed to view the data:

```
GRANT SELECT
        ON PRODUCT
        TO PUBLIC ;
```

A role can be allowed to modify data by:

```
GRANT UPDATE
        ON BONUSRATE
        TO VPSales ;
```

Granting The Power To Grant Privileges

This concept somewhat works like granting other users whom you trust with a little bit of your power to control the database access privileges. This actually makes a lot of sense especially if you are attempting to work with a large group. You can't always be around, sometimes you may fall sick and at that point you are going to need someone to temporarily take over!

This can be done using the grant option, the below is the example of the sales manager that has been given the power to provide the UPDATE privilege to others.

```
GRANT UPDATE (BonusPct)
        ON BONUSRATE
        TO SalesMgr
        WITH GRANT OPTION ;
GRANT UPDATE (BonusPct)
        ON BONUSRATE
        TO AsstSalesMgr ;
```

Take Away Privileges

As painful as the title suggests, sometimes you might be required to take crucial and serious steps in order to revoke a user from his/her privileges. And this is done by the REVOKE statement as follows:

```
REVOKE [GRANT OPTION FOR] privilege-list
          ON object
          FROM user-list [RESTRICT|CASCADE] ;
```

Understanding The Threats To Data Integrity

Now that you know how to control your structure, you should have a clear grasp of the most common threats which you might face that may hamper with your data stability.

- *Platform Instability:* Unexpected problems such as unseen bugs or problems in a new DBMS or operating system release falls under this category.
- *Equipment Failure:* This is, as the name implies, unforeseen events where your highly reliable state of the art equipment might fail sending your data to the afterlife. Keeping a redundancy backup which constantly copies everything will allow to protect against such an event.
- *The Problem Of Concurrent Access:* Even if you are completely sure that you program is free of

bugs and hardware errors, problem might still arise if multiple users are trying to access your database at the same time. In situations like this the system struggles to decide who gets to enter first (Contention). A good method to tackle against this is to invoke a serialization system where the first user is given access first, then the second and so on...

•

Techniques To Reduce Possibility Of Data Corruption

While there are several steps that you can take in order to make sure that your data are safe. Here are some of the more common ones that you should be familiar with:

- *The Usage Of SQL Transaction:* This is one of the prime method through which SQL maintains the database integrity. We have already discussed about this earlier. It simply encapsulates all of the SQL statement which may affect the database and are only carried out using the COMMIT or ROLLBACK option.

  Start of the application

Various SQL statements (SQL transaction-1)

COMMIT or ROLLBACK

Various SQL statements (SQL transaction-2)

COMMIT or ROLLBACK

Various SQL statements (SQL transaction-3)

COMMIT or ROLLBACK

End of the application

- *Isolation:* Another method is to isolate the individual transaction so that they are not conflicting with one another, even if multiple users are working at the same time. Using the SET TRANSACTION command, Isolation can very well lock up objects in the database if they are being fringed with in the wrong way.

SET TRANSACTION

READ ONLY,

```
                    ISOLATION LEVEL READ
UNCOMMITTED,
                    DIAGNOSTICS SIZE 4 ;
        SET TRANSACTION
                    READ WRITE,
                    ISOLATION LEVEL SERIALIZABLE,
                    DIAGNOSTICS SIZE 8 ;
```

- *Usage Of Savepoints:* Combining the ROLLBACK and SAVEPOINT statements, the flow of a transaction can be controlled. The SAVEPOINT is set up essentially to terminate a transaction. This gives you the opportunity to roll back to the last save point should any problem occur right after the former transaction has been made.

```
SAVEPOINT savepoint_name ;
```

To Rollback

```
ROLLBACK TO SAVEPOINT savepoint_name ;
```

8. Tables Modifying And Controlling

Altering table

The ALTER TABLE command is used to modify existing database tables. This is a powerful command that will let you change a table's name, add new fields, remove columns, edit field definitions, modify the table's storage values, and include or exclude constraints.

Here's the basic syntax for altering a table:

Changing a Table's Name

The ALTER TABLE command can be used with the RENAME function to change a table's name.

To demonstrate the use of this statement, you will use the EMPLOYEES table with the following records:

Assuming that you want to change the EMPLOYEES table name to INVESTORS, you can easily do so with this statement:

Your table is now named INVESTORS.

Modifying Column Attributes

A column's attributes refer to the properties and behaviors of data entered in a column. You will normally set the column attributes at the time you create the table. However, you may still change one or more attributes using the ALTER TABLE command.

You may modify the following:

- Column name
- Column Data type assigned to a column
- The scale, length, or precision of a column
- Use or non-use of NULL values in a column

Renaming Columns

You may want to modify a column's name to reflect the data that they contain. For instance, since you renamed the EMPLOYEES database to INVESTORS, the column name SALARY will no longer be appropriate. You can change the column name to something like CAPITAL. Likewise, you may want to change its data type from DECIMAL to an INTEGER TYPE with a maximum of ten digits.

Deleting a Column

The column Position is no longer applicable at this point. You can drop the column using this statement:

ALTER TABLE INVESTORS

DROP COLUMN Position;

Here's the updated INVESTORS table:

Adding a New Column

Since you're now working on a different set of data, you may decide to add another column to make the data on the INVESTORS table more relevant. You can add a column that will store the number of stocks owned by each investor. You may name the new column as STOCKS. This column will accept integers up to 9 digits.

You can use this statement to add the STOCKS column:

ALTER TABLE INVESTORS ADD STOCKS INT(9);

Here's the updated INVESTOR'S table:

Modifying an Existing Column without Changing its Name

You may also combine the ALTER TABLE command with the MODIFY keyword to change the data type and specifications of a table. To demonstrate, you can use the following statement to modify the data type of the column CAPITAL from an INT type to a DECIMAL type with up to 9 digits and two decimal numbers.

By this time, you may be curious to see the column names and attributes of the INVESTORS table. You can use the 'SHOW COLUMNS' statement to display the table's structure. Enter the following statement:

SHOW COLUMNS FROM INVESTORS;

Here's a screenshot of the result:

You will also get the same results with this statement:

DESC INVESTORS;

Rules to Remember when Using ALTER TABLE

- Adding Columns to a Database Table

When adding a new column, bear in mind that you can't add a column with a NOT NULL attribute to a table with existing data. You will generally specify a column to be NOT NULL to indicate that it will hold a value. Adding a NOT NULL column with contradict the constraint if the existing data don't have values for a new column.

- Modifying Fields/Columns

You should pay close attention to the following rules when modifying current database column:

1. You can easily modify the data type of a column.
2. You can always increase the length of a column but you may only decrease the length of a column if it is equal to or shorter than the desired column length.
3. You can increase the number of digits that numeric data types will hold but you will only be able to decrease it if the largest number of digits stored by a table is equal to or lower than the desired number of digits.
4. You can increase or decrease the decimal places of numeric data types as long as they don't exceed the maximum allowable decimal places.

Deleting and modifying tables can result to loss of valuable information if not handled properly. Hence, be extremely careful when you're executing the ALTER TABLE and DROP TABLE statements.

Deleting Tables

The DROP TABLE command is used to remove a table and its definitions from a database. Dropping a table will also remove its data, associated index, triggers, constraints, and permission data. You should be careful when using this statement.

Here's the syntax::

For example, if you want to delete the INVESTORS TABLE from the xyzcompany database, you may use this statement:

DROP TABLE INVESTORS;

The DROP TABLE command effectively removed the INVESTORS table from the current database.

If you try to access the INVESTORS table with this command:

SELECT* FROM INVESTORS;

SQL will return an error like this;

Combining and joining tables

You can combine data from several tables if a common field exists between them. The JOIN statement is used to perform this action.

SQL supports several types of JOIN operations:

INNER JOIN

The INNER JOIN, or simply JOIN, is the most commonly used type of JOIN. It displays the rows when the tables to be joined have a matching field.

Here's the syntax:

In this variation, the JOIN clause is used instead of INNER JOIN.

LEFT JOIN

The LEFT JOIN operation returns all left table rows with the matching right table rows. If no match is found, the right side returns NULL.

Here's the syntax for LEFT JOIN:

In some database systems, the keyword LEFT OUTER JOIN is used instead of LEFT JOIN. Here's the syntax for this variation:

RIGHT JOIN

This JOIN operation returns all right table rows with the matching left table rows. If no match is found, the left side returns NULL.

Here's the syntax for this operation:

In some database systems, the RIGHT OUTER JOIN is used instead of LEFT JOIN. Here's the syntax for this variation:

FULL OUTER JOIN

This JOIN operation will display all rows when at least one table meets the condition. It combines the results from both RIGHT and LEFT join operations.

Here's the syntax:

To demonstrate the JOIN operation in SQL, you will use the tables Branch_Sales and Branch_Location:

Branch_Sales Table

Branch	Product_ID	Sales
New York	101	7500.00
Los Angeles	102	6450.00
Chicago	101	1560.00

Philadelphia	101	1980.00
Denver	102	3500.00
Seattle	101	2500.00
Detroit	102	1450.00

Location Table

Region	Branch
East	New York City
East	Chicago
East	Philadelphia
East	Detroit
West	Los Angeles

West	Denver
West	Seattle

The objective is to fetch the sales by region. The Location table contains the data on regions and branches while the Branch_Sales table holds the sales data for each branch. To find the sales per region, you will need to combine the data from the Location and Branch_Sales tables. Notice that these tables have a common field, the Branch. This field links the two tables.

The following statement will demonstrate how you can link these two tables by using table aliases:

```
SELECT A1.Region Region, SUM(A2.Sales) Sales

FROM Location A1, Branch_Sales A2

WHERE A1.Branch = A2.Branch

GROUP BY A1.Region;
```

This would be the result:

In the first two lines, the statement tells SQL to select the fields 'Region' from the Location table and the total of the 'Sales' field from the Branch_Sales table. The statement uses table aliases. The 'Region' field was aliased as Region while the sum of the SALES field was aliased as SALES.

Table aliasing is the practice of using a temporary name for a table or a table column. Using aliases helps make statements more readable and concise. For example, if you opt not to use a table alias for the first line, you would have used the following statement to achieve the same result:

```
SELECT Location.Region Region,

SUM(Branch_Sales.Sales) SALES
```

Alternatively, you can specify a join between two tables by using the JOIN and ON keywords. For instance, using these keywords, the query would be:

```
SELECT A1.Region REGION, SUM(A2.Sales) SALES

FROM Location A1

JOIN Branch_Sales A2

ON A1.Branch = A2.Branch

GROUP BY A1.Region;
```

The query would produce an identical result:

Using Inner Join

An inner join displays rows when there is one or more matches on two tables. To demonstrate, you will use the following tables:

Branch_Sales table

Branch	Product_ID	Sales
New York	101	7500.00
Philadelphia	101	1980.00
Denver	102	3500.00
Seattle	101	2500.00
Detroit	102	1450.00

Location_table

Region	Branch
East	New York
East	Chicago
East	Philadelphia
East	Detroit
West	Los Angeles
West	Denver
West	Seattle

The objective of the query is to fetch the sales data per branch and only for branches that are listed in the Branch_Sales table. You can achieve this by using the INNER JOIN statement.

You can enter the following:

SELECT A1.Branch BRANCH, SUM(A2.Sales) SALES

FROM Location A1

```
INNER JOIN Branch_Sales A2
ON A1.Branch = A2.Branch
GROUP BY A1.Branch;
```

This would be the result:

Take note that by using the INNER JOIN, only the branches with records in the Branch_Sales report were included in the results even though you are actually applying the SELECT statement on the Location table. The 'Chicago' and 'Los Angeles' branches were excluded because there are no records for these branches in the Branch_Sales table.

Using Outer Join

In the previous example, you have used the Inner Join to combine tables with common rows. In some cases, you may need to select all elements of a table whether or not they have a matching record in the second table. The OUTER JOIN command is used for this purpose.

The example for the OUTER JOIN will use the same tables used for INNER JOIN: the Branch_Sales table and Location_table.

This time, you want a list of sales figures for all stores. A regular join would have excluded Chicago and Los Angeles because these branches were not part of the Branch_Sales table. You will want, therefore, to do an OUTER JOIN.

Here's the statement:

```
SELECT A1.Branch, SUM(A2.Sales) SALES

FROM Location A1, Branch_Sales A2

WHERE A1.Branch = A2.Branch (+)

GROUP BY A1.Branch;
```

Take note that the Outer Join syntax is database-dependent. The above statement uses the Oracle syntax.

Here's the result:

When combining tables, be aware that some JOIN syntax will have different results across database systems. To maximize this powerful database feature, it is imporant to read the RDBMS documentation.

9. Aggregate Functions, Delete, & Update

Up till now, we have been dealing with individual records. We saw how to insert individual records in a database, how to retrieve records from the database based on criteria, and how to apply different types of filters to fetch a desired output. What if we want to retrieve the maximum age of the patients from the PatientAge column? SQL Aggregate functions help us perform this task. We shall see some of the most commonly used aggregate functions in SQL. We shall also see how we can delete records from a table and how we can update existing records.

Contents

- **Aggregate Functions**

1. Count()
2. Avg()
3. Sum()
4. Max()
5. Min()
6. First/Top()
7. Ucase/Upper()
8. Lcase/Lower()

- **Delete Statement**
- **Update Statement**

1- Aggregate Functions

The following are some of the most commonly used functions.

1. Count()

The Count() function counts the number of rows which satisfy a particular criteria. For instance, if you want to count the number of patients who have Heart disease, you can use Count() function as follows:

Query 1

```
SELECT COUNT(PatientID) as PatientsWithHeartDisease

From Patient
WHERE DiseaseDescription LIKE ('%heart%')
```

The above query counts the patient with heart disease and displays the result in the "PatientsWithHeartDisease" column.

2. Avg()

The Avg() function returns the average of values in a particular table column based on some criteria. For instance, if you want to retrieve the average age of all patients with heart disease, you can employ the Avg() function as follows:

Query 2

```
SELECT AVG(PatientAge) as AverageAgeofHeartDisease

From Patient
WHERE DiseaseDescription LIKE ('%heart%')
```

3. Sum()

The Sum() function returns the sum of the values in a particular table column based on some criteria. For instance, if you want to retrieve the sum of the ages of all patients, you can employ the Sum() function as follows:

Query 3

```
SELECT Sum(PatientAge) as SumOfAges
From Patient
```

4. Max()

The Max() function returns the maximum of all of the values in a particular table column. For instance, if you want to retrieve the maximum age of all the patients, you can use the Max() function as follows:

Query 4

```
SELECT Max(PatientAge) as MaximumAge
From Patient
```

5. Min()

Similarly, to retrieve the minimum patient age, the following query can be executed:

Query 5

```
SELECT Min(PatientAge) as MaximumAge
From Patient
```

6. Top/First()

The Top() or First() functions return the top 'n' of all of the values in a particular table column, where "n" is any integer. For instance, if you want to retrieve the age of the first three patients in the "Patient" table, you can use the Top() function as follows:

Query 6

```
SELECT Top 3 PatientAge as First3Ages
From Patient
```

The above query will retrieve the ages of the first three patients. The output will look like this:

First3Ages
10
26
15

To retrieve the ages of the last three patients in the "Patient" table, you can use the Top() query in conjunction with the "Order By" clause as follows:

Query 7

```
SELECT Top 3 PatientAge as Last3Ages
From Patient Order by PatientAge desc
```

The output of Query 7 is as follows:

Last3Ages

47
42
31

7. Upper()/Ucase

The Upper() or Ucase() function converts all the values in the selected column to uppercase. This function applies only to columns with string or character values.

Query 8

```
SELECT Upper(PatientName) as PatientNameUpper

From Patient
```

The output of Query 8 is as follows:

PatientNameUpper
JAMES
JOSEPH

SARAH
JULIAN
ISAAC
MARGRET
MIKE
RUSS
MARIA
CANDICE

8. Lcase()/Lower()

Similarly, to convert column values to lower case, the Lcase() or Lower() function is used. Since I am using MS SQL Server for demonstration purposes, I will use Lower() in my Query.

Query 9

```
SELECT Lower(PatientName) as PatientNameLower
From Patient
```

The output will contain all the PatientName values in lower case as follows:

PatientNameLower
james
joseph
sarah
julian
isaac
margret
mike
russ
maria
candice

Delete Statement

We know how to insert records into a database; we also know how to retrieve records using a SELECT statement and how to filter records using a "where" clause with various SQL operators. Now we will learn how to delete records from the table.

To delete records, the SQL DELETE statement is used. Like the SELECT statement, the DELETE statement can also be used in conjunction with a SELECT statement to delete filtered records. Let's look at how we can delete all the records from the table. To do so, the following query can be executed:

Query 10

```
DELETE From Patient
```

This query will delete all the records from the patient table. However, in some scenarios, we want only records that satisfy particular criteria to be deleted. For instance, you can delete the records of all patients with heart disease using the following query:

Query 11

```
Delete From Patient
where DiseaseDescription like('%heart%')
```

The above query will delete all the patient records which have heart disease in the DiseaseDescription column.

3- Update Statement

We know how to insert, retrieve, and delete records; in this section, we shall learn how to update an existing record. To update a record, the UPDATE statement is used in SQL, followed by the SET keyword, which is used to update an existing value.

If you want to replace the string "Heart Disease" in the DiseaseDescription column with the string "Cardiac Disease", you can use an UPDATE statement as follows:

Query 12

```
UPDATE Patient
SET DiseaseDescription = 'Cardiac Disease'
where DiseaseDescription like('%heart%')
```

Exercise 7

Task:

Delete the records of all patients aged greater than 30 who have ear diseases. Set the age of all patients with lung disease to 40.

Solution

Deleting Records

```
Delete From Patient
where PatientAge > 30 AND DiseaseDescription LIKE
('%ear%')
```

Updating Records

```
UPDATE Patient
set PatientAge = 40
  where DiseaseDescription LIKE ('%lung%')
```

10. Relationships & Join Queries

Up to this point, we have been executing all our queries on a single table. However, real life databases contain hundreds, or even thousands, of tables. These tables are associated with each other via relationships. We saw how the "Student" table was associated with the "Department" table via a column, DID, which stored the ID of the department to which student belonged. This is one type of database relationship. In this chapter, we shall study different types of database relationships and Join queries.

Contents

- **Table Relationships**

1. **One-to-One Relationship**
2. **One-to-Many Relationship**
3. **Many-to-Many Relationship**

- **Join Statements**

1. **Inner Join**
2. **Left Join**
3. **Right Join**
4. **Outer Join**

- **Group By**
- **Having**

1- Table Relationships

Database tables can be linked with each other via one of the three types of relationships.

- **One-to-One Relationship**

In a "one-to-one" relationship between two tables, for every record in the first table, there is exactly one record in the second table. The Primary key of the first table exists as the Foreign key in the second table and vice versa. For example, there is a "one-to-one" relationship between the "Employee" table and the "Pension" table, since one Pension record belongs to one Employee and one Employee can have only one Pension record. In most scenarios, "one-to-one" relationships are removed by merging the data into a single column.

Note:

A Foreign key is basically a column in the table which stores the primary key of the table with which it is linked. In we saw that the Student table had a column labeled DID, which stored the ID of the department to which a student belonged.

- **One-to-Many Relationship**

In a "one-to-many" relationship, against one record in the first table, there can be multiple records in the second table. In a "one-to-many" relationship, the table on the "many" side of the relationship is stored as a Foreign key and the Primary key of the table is on the "one" side of the relationship. The relationship between the "Department" and "Student" tables is the perfect example of a "one-to-many" relationship, since one department can have multiple students. In the "Student" table, many records can have one department.

- **Many-to-Many Relationships**

In "many-to-many" relationships, for one record in the first table, there can be multiple records in the second table; for one record in the second table, there can be multiple records in the first table. The relationship between the "Author" and "Book" tables is a good example of "many-to-many" relationships. A book can be written by multiple authors while an author can write multiple books. In most cases, "many-to-many" relationships are broken down into "one-to-many" relationships by creating an intermediate table that has "one-to-many" relationships with both the actual tables.

2- Join Statements

Join statements are used to select column values from two or more tables which are linked with each other. For instance, take a scenario where you have to display the names of students along with the names of the departments to which they belong. However, there is no department name column in the "Student" table; it only contains the department ID, which serves as a Foreign key to Department. Therefore, we need some mechanism to select column values from multiple tables which are linked together. JOIN queries help us perform this function.

Before executing JOIN queries, run the following script in your query window.

Script 1

```
Create Database School

Use School
```

```
Go
CREATE TABLE Student
  (StudID int PRIMARY KEY NOT NULL,
   StudName varchar(50) NOT NULL,
   StudentAge int NULL,
   StudentGender varchar(10) NOT NULL,
           DepID int NULL)
CREATE TABLE Department
  (DepID int PRIMARY KEY NOT NULL,
   DepName varchar(50) NOT NULL,
           DepCapacity int NULL)
ALTER TABLE Student ADD CONSTRAINT StudDepRel
FOREIGN KEY ( DepID) references Department(DepID)
INSERT INTO Department Values
(1, 'English', 100),
(2, 'Math', 80),
(3, 'History', 70),
(4, 'French', 90),
(5, 'Geography', 100),
(6, 'Drawing', 150),
(7, 'Architecture', 120)
INSERT INTO Student Values
(1, 'Alice', 21, 'Male', 2),
(2, 'Alfred', 20, 'Male', 3),
```

```
(3, 'Henry', 19, 'Male', 3),
(4, 'Jacobs', 22, 'Male', 5),
(5, 'Bob', 20, 'Male', 4),
(6, 'Shane', 22, 'Male', 4),
(7, 'Linda', 24, 'Female', 4),
(8, 'Stacy', 20, 'Female', 1),
(9, 'Wolfred', 21, 'Male', 2),
(10, 'Sandy', 25, 'Female', 1),
(11, 'Colin', 18, 'Male', 1),
(12, 'Maria', 19, 'Female', 3),
(13, 'Ziva', 20, 'Female', 5),
(14, 'Mark', 23, 'Male', 5),
(15, 'Fred', 25, 'Male', 2),
(16, 'Vic', 25, 'Male',null),
(17, 'Nick', 25, 'Male',null)
```

The above script will create a new database, School, with two tables, "Department" and "Student". A "one-to-many" relationship has been defined between the "Department" and

"Student" tables using following query:

```
ALTER TABLE Student ADD CONSTRAINT StudDepRel
FOREIGN KEY ( DepID) references Department(DepID)
```

The above query states that, in the Student column, a Foreign key constraint named "StudDepRel" (you can use any name) will be added, which sets the DepID column of the Student table as a Foreign key which references the DepID column of the Department table.

After you run Script 1, you should have "Department" and "Student" tables containing following data:

Department Table

DepID	**DepName**	**DepCapacity**
1	English	100
2	Math	80
3	History	70
4	French	90
5	Geography	100
6	Drawing	150
7	Architecture	120

Student Table

StudID	StudName	StudentAge	StudentGender	DepID
1	Alice	21	Male	2
2	Alfred	20	Male	3
3	Henry	19	Male	3
4	Jacobs	22	Male	5
5	Bob	20	Male	4
6	Shane	22	Male	4
7	Linda	24	Female	4
8	Stacy	20	Female	1
9	Wolfred	21	Male	2
10	Sandy	25	Female	1
11	Colin	18	Male	1
12	Maria	19	Female	3
13	Ziva	20	Female	5
14	Mark	23	Male	5
15	Fred	25	Male	2
16	Vic	25	Male	NULL
17	Nick	25	Male	NULL

- INNER JOIN

INNER JOIN (also called JOIN) retrieves data from the selected column from both tables if, and only if, there exists a common value in both tables in the column specified by the JOIN condition. For instance, to retrieve the names of students from the student column along with their department names from the department column, the following INNER JOIN query is used:

Query 1

```
SELECT Student.StudName, Department.DepName

From Student
Join Department
On Student.DepID = Department.DepID
```

The output of the above query is as follows:

StudName	DepName
Alice	Math
Alfred	History
Henry	History
Jacobs	Geography
Bob	French
Shane	French
Linda	French
Stacy	English
Wolfred	Math

Sandy	English
Colin	English
Maria	History
Ziva	Geography
Mark	Geography
Fred	Math

You can see only those records from the "Student" and "Department" tables have been retrieved where there was a common value in the DepID of the "Student" table and the DepID of the "Department" table. The last two records from the "Student" table have not been retrieved, since there is no corresponding DepID. Similarly, the last two records from the "Department" table have also not been retrieved, since they are not referenced by any of the records in the "Student" table.

- **LEFT JOIN**

LEFT JOIN retrieves all the records from the first table and only those records from the second table where a common value exists in both tables, as specified by the JOIN condition. For instance, the following query retrieves all the records from the "Student" table and only those records from the "Department" table where there is a corresponding DepID value in the "Student" table.

Query 2

```
SELECT Student.StudName, Department.DepName

From Student
Left Join Department
On Student.DepID = Department.DepID
```

The output of Query 2 is as follows:

StudName	*DepName*
Alice	**Math**
Alfred	**History**
Henry	**History**
Jacobs	**Geography**
Bob	**French**
Shane	**French**

Linda	**French**
Stacy	**English**
Wolfred	**Math**
Sandy	**English**
Colin	**English**
Maria	**History**
Ziva	**Geography**
Mark	**Geography**
Fred	**Math**
Vic	**NULL**
Nick	**NULL**

You can see that the last two students don't have any corresponding DepID, yet they have been retrieved.

- **RIGHT JOIN**

RIGHT JOIN retrieves all the records from the second table and only those records from the first table where a common value exists in both tables, as specified by the JOIN condition. For instance, the following query retrieves all the records from the "Department" table and only those records from the "Student" table where there is a corresponding DepID value in the "Department" table.

Query 3

```
SELECT Student.StudName, Department.DepName

From Student
Right Join Department
On Student.DepID = Department.DepID
```

StudName	**DepName**
Stacy	*English*
Sandy	*English*
Colin	*English*
Alice	*Math*

Wolfred	Math
Fred	Math
Alfred	History
Henry	History
Maria	History
Bob	French
Shane	French
Linda	French
Jacobs	Geography
Ziva	Geography
Mark	Geography
NULL	Drawing
NULL	Architecture

- **FULL JOIN**

FULL JOIN is the union of RIGHT JOIN and LEFT JOIN. FULL JOIN retrieves all records from both tables, whether or not a match is found between the Foreign key and Primary key of the linked table. Have a look at the following query:

Query 4

```
SELECT Student.StudName, Department.DepName

From Student
Full Join Department
On Student.DepID = Department.DepID
```

The output of the code in Query 4 is as follows:

StudName	DepName
Alice	Math
Alfred	History
Henry	History
Jacobs	Geography
Bob	French
Shane	French

Linda	French
Stacy	English
Wolfred	Math
Sandy	English
Colin	English
Maria	History
Ziva	Geography
Mark	Geography
Fred	Math
Vic	NULL
Nick	NULL
NULL	Drawing
NULL	Architecture

3- Group By

The "Group By" statement allows us to group data based on results from some aggregate functions. For instance, if you want to display the name of each department along with the average age of the student from that department, you can use a "Group By" statement as follows:

Query 5

```
SELECT                              Department.DepName,
AVG(Student.StudentAge) as AverageStudentAge

 From Student
 Right Join Department
 On Student.DepID = Department.DepID
 Group by DepName
```

The above query will calculate the average age of students belonging to each department and will display them against each department's name.

DepName	AverageStudentAge
Architecture	NULL
Drawing	NULL
English	21
French	22
Geography	21
History	19
Math	22

4- HAVING

Since a "Where" clause cannot be used to filter data grouped by aggregate functions, the "Having" statement was introduced in the SQL. For instance, if you want to retrieve the names of only those departments where the average age of students is greater than 20, you can use a "Having" statement as follows:

Query 6

```
SELECT Department.DepName, AVG(Student.StudentAge) as AverageStudentAge

 From Student
Right Join Department
 On Student.DepID = Department.DepID
 Group by DepName
 Having AVG(Student.StudentAge) > 20
```

The result of Query 6 is as follows:

DepName	AverageStudentAge
English	21
French	22
Geography	21
Math	22

Exercise 8

Task:

For each department, display the department name and maximum age of students in that department if the age is between 21 and 24.

Solution

```
SELECT Department.DepName,
Max(Student.StudentAge) as Age
 From Student
Right Join Department
 On Student.DepID = Department.DepID
 Group by DepName
 Having Max(Student.StudentAge) Between 21 AND 24
```

11. Expressions

When operators, functions and values are used together in such a manner that the same can be evaluated to compute a value, this combination is referred to as an expression. You can visualize SQL expression as a mathematical formula that is written using the SQL syntax. In order to help you understand how a typical SQL expression looks like, let us take an example.

SELECT col1, col2, colN FROM t_name WHERE [exp];

In the given example, the expression is performing a SELECT operation and requests selection of columns 1 to N from the table 't_name'. The results corresponding to rows for which the given expression evaluates to true must be outputted. SQL supports three types of expressions, each of which has been discussed below.

Boolean Expressions

In case of boolean expressions, fetching of data is done after a single value is matched. The syntax for such expressions is as follows –

SELECT col1, col2, colN FROM t_name WHERE exp_matching_single_value;

This statement selects columns 1 to N from the table 't_name' and outputs the rows that satisfy the condition specified by exp_matching_single_value. In order to gain better understanding of boolean expressions, let us take an example. Consider a table named CUSTOMERS. The SQL statement given below shall print all the records available in the CUSTOMERS table.

*SELECT * FROM CUSTOMERS;*

The output will typically look like –

ID	Name	Age	Salary
98701	Rohan	45	50000.00
98675	Amit	32	37000.00
98706	Shayla	22	12000.00
98718	Mathews	37	41000.00

The following SQL statement is the simplest example of a boolean expression.

SELECT * FROM CUSTOMERS WHERE Salary=37000;

The execution of this query will return the following.

ID	Name	Age	Salary
98675	Amit	32	37000.00

Numeric Expression

Expressions that are of the numeric type are typically used to perform mathematical operations in a SQL statement. Syntax for numeric expressions is as follows –

SELECT formula_arith as Op_Name [FROM t_name WHERE cond];

Here formula_arith is any mathematical formula that can be specified to perform an arithmetic operation in the SQL query. Besides this, t_name is the name of the table and cond is the condition of the WHERE clause. A simple example to demonstrate the working of numeric expressions is given below –

SELECT (100+76) AS ADD;

Execution of this query shall give the result 176. Many other SQL functions like sum(), avg() and count, in addition to many others, may be used as formula_arith to perform data calculations against the values selected from the columns of the table concerned. For example, the SQL statement given below shall count the number of entries in the CUSTOMERS table.

SELECT count(*) FROM CUSTOMERS;

Execution of this query will return the value 4.

Date Expressions

Such expressions are typically used to get information about the current date or time on the system. Functions like GETDATE() or CURRENT_TIMESTAMP may be used in the SQL query to get the desired results. Sample statements for their usage have been given below –

SELECT CURRENT_TIMESTAMP;
SELECT GETDATE();

12. Sequences & Injection

Make sure you've understood the rest of this book before moving onto this chapter. In it we will be discussing some of the most complex elements of SQL, such as increments, and injections. If you're having trouble with this chapter, don't worry too much, it's the most difficult, and effort-intensive part of the book. Without further ado, let's dive in!

Increments

Increments are possible in SQL. For the uninitiated, to increment a value means to increase it by a given number. Usually, this number is one, and usually, the value is an integer.

SQL's AUTO-INCREMENT function allows you to automatically increase a number by one every time it is invoked. Now, this may seem a bit foreign at first. That's why we'll give you a general example of how the SQL AUTO INCREMENT function is generally used.

CREATE TABLE Table1

```
(
ID int NOT NULL AUTO_INCREMENT,
Name varchar(200) NOT NULL,
Title varchar(200),
Location varchar(200),
Country varchar(255),
PRIMARY KEY (ID)
)
```

This is an excellent example of how SQL performs increments. When it comes to dialects like MySQL, replacements like AUTO_INCREMENT also exist. According to default, the starting value, if left undeclared, will be presumed to be 1, and will be incremented by 1 every time the loop is run.

If 1 is not the desired value you want to start with, use the following syntax:

```
ALTER TABLE Table1 AUTO_INCREMENT=X
```

Where X is the number you want to increment by. If you're trying to start a new data point in say, table 1, then you won't need to specify for every value.

For example, let's suppose Table 1 contains some sort of people, with a name and the title. Take a gander at this SQL snippet:

```
INSERT INTO Students (Name,Title)

VALUES ('Ilija','Mr')
```

This statement will make a brand new data point in the table table1, and will insert a person named Ilija with the prefix Mr. Naturally, these columns will be changed to reflect this.

Renumbering and Starting At A Value

Now, this was addressed in a minor way previously, however, there are multiple ways to start the numbering at a certain value, and increment by a larger, or lower number as you see fit.

This can be quite useful, for example, when you're grading students, you only need different scores in increments of say 10 points, so you could easily write a program that auto-fills every student into a grade by their scores.

In general, this is one of the easier features of SQL to learn. This is the syntax for incrementing at a larger starting value, and with a number N:

```
CREATE TABLE Table1

(

ID int 10 AUTO_INCREMENT,

Name varchar(200) NOT NULL,

Title varchar(200),

Location varchar(200),

Country varchar(255),

PRIMARY KEY (ID)

)

ALTER TABLE Table1 AUTO_INCREMENT=N
```

Easy isn't it? Great! Now move on and give your own attempts a try, let your imagination run wild on it.

Stopping SQL Injection

Now, SQL injection is one of the most common mistakes beginner SQL developers make. We'll try to teach you how to prevent this security issue from happening to you in this section, although these are the basics and you could easily write another whole book purely on this subject.

Generally, injection will happen when you take user input through a webpage. After this is inserted into the SQL database, there is a variety of things that can happen. Heck, you might accidentally get an SQL statement that will straight-up run through your database.

This means it's extremely easy to insert a virus through your webpage, as they might give you an SQL command instead of say, their name, or their order. When this happens, it can have disastrous consequences. This is generally restricted by limiting what your users can input. For example, the following script limits the number of characters that can be used for ordering to being between 6 and 40.

```
if (found_match("/^\w{4,40}$/", $_GET['order'],
$matches)) {

  $result = mysql_query("SELECT * FROM BUYS

    WHERE name = $matches[false]");

} else {

  echo " You have entered an invalid order";
```

}

If you're wondering how exactly people can do this, let's presume a user gives this input:

```
$name= "A"; DELETE FROM BUYS;

mysql_query( "SELECT FROM BUYS WHERE
order='{$order}')
```

Now this, when processed, will run the query that was inserted in the 'order' field. This query, as you can see, will straight-up delete every order you have. Imagine a business having to recover from all of their orders being entirely lost? That's right, they don't like that very much, and their SQL dev is probably getting fired.

With that being said, most modern SQL derivatives like MySQL don't allow you to stack SQL functions. This is good because it leads to failure if the user tries to do something like that.

One of the few saving graces of MySQL, is that it will ban every myql_query() call that is stacked within another one. This helps save you from SQL injections.

Other PHP-based database extensions aren't quite so kind. SQLite for example, will happily let your users stack their queries, and execute everything told to them. This is part of the reason why they are generally not used by large companies.

13. Creating Databases and Definition Table Relationships

In this book we will follow a step by step approach to explain different SQL concepts. We shall start with Entity Relationship Diagram (ERD) which serves as blue print for the database. ERD defines database scheme. We will then create our database according to that scheme. The next step will be to add some data in the database. Once we have a database with some data in it we are good to experiment with it. So let's start with ERD.

Entity Relationship Diagram (ERD)

ERD is the graphical representation of database scheme. ERD contains tables in the database, the columns within those tables and relationships between the tables.

The database that we are going to develop in this book is a Hospital database. It will contain six tables: Patients, Treatment, Doctors Examinations,

Patient_Examination and Patient_Visits. Figure 2.1 contains ERD for the hospital database.

The Hospital database ERD contains all the tables in the hospital database along with their relationship. These relationships will be explained later in this chapter.

Creating a Database

We have an ERD, now we must actually create our database as defined by ERD. Let's execute our first query of the book. This query will create database on the database server.

CREATE DATABASE Hospital;

The syntax of CREATE database query is very simple, you have to use the keyword CREATE DATABASE followed by the name of the database. You can give any name to your database.

Note:

It is also important to mention here that SQL is case insensitive. It is also worth mentioning that we are using MS SQL Server 2017 as our DBMS in this book. You can use any other relational database system such as MySQL, SQL Lite etc. The core SQL is similar for all the databases with only slight variations.

You could write the above query as follows:

Create database Hospital;

There will be no difference.

Deleting a Database

To delete existing database we use DROP DATABASE query. For instance if you want to delete Hospital database that we created, execute the following query:

DROP DATABASE Hospital;

Before moving forward, recreate the Hospital database if you have deleted it, since in the next section we are going to create tables within the Hospital database.

Creating a Table

We have created Hospital database but it is empty at the moment. There is no data in the database. Databases store data in tables. Therefore the first step after creating database is to create tables.

As a rule of thumb, create all the independent tables first and then the dependent tables. A table is independent if does not contain any foreign key and vice versa. The relationships between the tables define dependency and independency of tables.

If we look at the ERD Patients, Doctors and Examinations tables are independent table because they do not contain any foreign key. Therefore we will create these tables first. The syntax for creating a table is as follows:

CREATE TABLE table_name

(

Colum1_name data_type constraints,

Colum2_name data_type constraints,

)

Now let's create Patients table using this syntax. Execute the following query on your database server to create Patient table.

USE Hospital;

CREATE Table Patients

```
(
Id int IDENTITY (1,1) PRIMARY KEY NOT NULL,
name VARCHAR (50) NOT NULL,
age int NOT NULL,
gender VARCHAR (50) NOT NULL,
blood_group VARCHAR (50),
phone BIGINT
);
```

The first line in the above query is USE Hospital. The USE command is used to specify the database in which you are creating your database. We are creating Patients table inside the Hospital database, therefore mentioned it via USE command.

Look how we defined columns inside the Patients table. To define a column we start with the column name, followed by the type of the data stored by the column and the constraints upon the key column. For instance the first column inside the Patients is the 'id' column. The third part of the column definition is the constraint specifications. A constraint implements certain rules on table columns. The id column has three constraints:

- IDENTITY: THAT DATA WILL BE AUTOMATICALLY ADDED TO THIS COLUMN

STARTING FROM ONE AND IT WILL BE INCREMENTED BY 1 FOR EACH NEW RECORD.

- PRIMARY KEY: SPECIFIES THAT THIS COLUMN IS THE PRIMARY KEY COLUMN?

- NOT NULL: Column cannot hold null values

Notice that the columns in the Patients table corresponds to those defined for the Patient table in the ERD.

Similarly create Doctors and Examinations tables using following queries:

USE Hospital

CREATE Table Doctors

(

Id int IDENTITY (1,1) PRIMARY KEY NOT NULL,
name VARCHAR (50) NOT NULL,
designition VARCHAR (50),
specialization VARCHAR (50),

);

USE Hospital
CREATE Table Examinations

```
(
id int IDENTITY (1,1) PRIMARY KEY NOT NULL,
name VARCHAR (50) NOT NULL,
price int NOT NULL,
);
```

We have created all the three independent tables. The next step is to create dependent tables i.e. Patient_Examination, Treatments and Patient_Visits table. These tables are bound in a relationship to the Patients table. Before creating these tables, let us first study the type of relationships that database tables can have.

Table Relationships

There are three major types of relationships between tables in a relational database:

- One to One Relation
- One to Many Relation
- Many to Many Relation

One to One Relation

In a one to one relation, for a record in the first table, there can be one and only one record in the related or dependent table. A simple example of one to relation is the relation between patient and his contact info. A patient can have one contact info, while particular contact info belongs to one patient. One to one relations are avoided in most of the cases and the tables participating in one to one relation are merged together. For instance you can have patient info e.g. name, last name, date of birth and contact info e.g. phone, address, email in a single table.

One to Many Relation

In one to many relation, each record in the first table can be referenced by multiple records in the second table. For instance in our Hospital database, Patients and Patient_Visits tables have one to many relationships with each other. For each record in the Patients table, there can be multiple records in the Patient_Visits table. In simple terms, a patient can have multiple visits to a hospital; however one visit belongs to only belongs to one Person.

To implement one to many relation in the database, we have to add a foreign key in the table that is on the "many" side of the relationship. This foreign key references the primary key of the table that is on the "one" side of the relationship. In the case of Patients and Patient_Visits tables, the latter will have a foreign key column that references the primary key of the former table. Let's implement it using a query.

```
USE Hospital

CREATE Table Patient_Visits (
id int IDENTITY(1,1) PRIMARY KEY NOT NULL,
patient_id int FOREIGN KEY REFERENCES Patients(id),
visit_time DATETIME NOT NULL
);
```

The above script creates Patient_Visits table in the Hospital database. It also implements one to many relation between Patient and Patient_Visits table. Take a look at the following line of code from the above script:

```
patient_id int FOREIGN KEY REFERENCES Patients(id),
```

This creates a foreign key column patient_id in the Patient_Visits table. This column references the id column of the Patients table. This is how we actually implement one to many relationships in the database.

Many to Many Relation

In many to many relation, each record in the first table can be referenced by multiple records in the second table. Similarly each record in the second table can be referenced by multiple records in the first table. For instance one patient can have multiple examinations; similarly one examination can be undertaken by multiple patients. In other words, for each record in the Patients table, there can be multiple records in the Patient_Examination table and vice versa.

Many to many relations are usually broken down into two one to many relations using a junction table. Both the tables involved in the many to many relation have one to many relation with the junction table. Junction table has foreign keys from all the tables involved in many to many relation. In the ERD for Hospital table we have defined Patient_Examination table as junction table to implement one to many relation between Patients and Examinations table. This Patient_Examination table will have two foreign keys: One that references the primary key column of the Patients table and the other that references the primary key column of the Examinations table. The following script creates Patient_Examination table in the hospital database.

CREATE Table Patient_Examination(

id int IDENTITY(1,1) PRIMARY KEY NOT NULL,

```
patient_id int FOREIGN KEY REFERENCES Patients(id),
examination_id int FOREIGN KEY REFERENCES
Examinations(id),
result VARCHAR(50)

);
```

Similarly Patients and Doctors also have one to many relation between them since a patient can be treated by many doctors and one doctor can treat many doctors. Here Treatments table is the junction table that implements the relation between Patient and Doctors table. The script for creating Treatments table is as follows:

```
CREATE Table Treatment(
id int IDENTITY(1,1) PRIMARY KEY NOT NULL,
patient_id int FOREIGN KEY REFERENCES Patients(id),
doctor_id int FOREIGN KEY REFERENCES Doctors(id),
remarks VARCHAR(50)
);
```

14. Filtering with Operators, Sorting with ORDER BY

In this chapter we are going to see, how we can filter data using different types of SQL operators in conjunction with the WHERE clause.

SQL Operators

There are four major types of operators in SQL:

- Comparison Operators
- Conjunctive Operators
- Logical Operators
- Negation Operators

The WHERE Clause

Before studying SQL operators in detail, first we need to understand WHERE clause. The WHERE clause filters records based on the operator used in the query. The syntax of WHERE clause is simple. Let's see a simple example of WHERE clause. This query filters all those patient records where id is greater than 5.

```
SELECT * FROM Patients
 WHERE id > 5
```

The output of the above query is as follows:

name	age	gender	blood_group	phone
Julie	26	Female	A+	12478963
Frank	35	Male	A-	85473216
Alex	21	Male	AB-	46971235
Hales	54	Male	B+	74698125
Elice	32	Female	O+	34169872

Now, let's study each SQL Operator in detail.

Comparison Operators

SQL comparison operators can be further divided into six types. These operators filter records by comparing values of the operands.

- EQUALITY (=)
- NON-EQUALITY (<>)
- LESS THAN VALUES (<)
- GREATER THAN VALUES (>)

- LESS THAN EQUAL TO (<=)
- Greater than equal to(>=)

The working principle of each of these operators has been demonstrated by examples. Take a look at them.

Equality Operator (=)

```
SELECT * FROM Patients

 WHERE name = 'Frank'
```

The above query returns record of the patient named 'Frank'.

Non-Equality (!=)

```
SELECT * FROM Patients

WHERE name != 'Frank'
```

The above query returns records of all the patients except the one named 'Frank'.

Less Than (<)

```
UPDATE Examinations

SET price = price * 1.1

 WHERE price < 250
```

The above query updates the price column of those records in the Examinations table where price is less than 250.

Greater Than (>)

```
SELECT * FROM Patients

 WHERE id > 5
```

Less than Equal To (<=)

```
SELECT * FROM Patients

 WHERE age <= 30
```

The above query selects all the records from Patients table where age is less than or equal to 30. The output of the above query will look like this:

id	name	age	gender	blood_group	phone
1	Tom	20	Male	O+	123589746
3	James	16	Male	O-	78452369
5	Sal	24	Male	O+	48963214
6	Julie	26	Female	A+	12478963
8	Alex	21	Male	AB-	46971235

Greater than Equal To (>=)

```
SELECT * FROM Patients
 WHERE age >= 30
```

The above query selects all the records from Patients table where age is greater than or equal to 30. The output of the above query will look like this:

id	name	age	gender	blood_group	phone
2	Kimer	45	Female	AB+	45686412
4	Matty	43	Female	B+	15789634
7	Frank	35	Male	A-	85473216
9	Hales	54	Male	B+	74698125
10	Elice	32	Female	O+	34169872

Conjunctive Operators

In the previous examples we used only one operator to filter data. If we want to filter records that satisfy multiple conditions, we can use Conjunctive operators.

There are two commonly used conjunctive operators in SQL.

- AND
- OR

Let's see both of them in action:

AND

SELECT * FROM Patients

WHERE age > 30 AND gender = 'Female'

The above query will retrieve records of all the patients with age greater than 30 and gender Female. The output of the above query will look like this:

id	name	age	gender	blood_group	phone
2	Kimer	45	Female	AB+	45686412
4	Matty	43	Female	B+	15789634
10	Elice	32	Female	O+	34169872

OR

SELECT * FROM Patients

WHERE age > 30 OR gender = 'Female'

This query will select records of all patients with either age greater than 30 or gender Female. The output of the above query will be:

id	name	age	gender	blood_group	phone
2	Kimer	45	Female	AB+	45686412
4	Matty	43	Female	B+	15789634
6	Julie	26	Female	A+	12478963
7	Frank	35	Male	A-	85473216
9	Hales	54	Male	B+	74698125
10	Elice	32	Female	O+	34169872

Logical Operators

Following are the most commonly used logical operators in SQL:

- IN
- BETWEEN
- LIKE
- DISTINCT

- IS NULL

IN

The IN operator is used to filter records based on the values specified in the IN operator. The IN operator takes comma separated values inside parenthesis as input. For instance if you want to retrieve records of all the patients whose blood group is O+ or O-, you can use IN operator as follows:

```
SELECT * FROM Patients
 WHERE blood_groupIN('O+','O-')
```

The output of the above query will be records of all the patients with blood group O+ or O- as shown below:

id	name	age	gender	blood_group	phone
1	Tom	20	Male	O+	123589746
3	James	16	Male	O-	78452369
5	Sal	24	Male	O+	48963214
10	Elice	32	Female	O+	34169872

BETWEEN

BETWEEN operators filter records that falls between specified ranges. The range is specified using AND operator. For instance if you want to retrieve records of all the patients with id between 3 and 7, you can use BETWEEN operator as follows:

```
SELECT * FROM Patients
 WHERE id BETWEEN 3 AND 7
```

The output of the above query will look be:

id	name	age	gender	blood_group	phone
3	James	16	Male	O-	78452369
4	Matty	43	Female	B+	15789634
5	Sal	24	Male	O+	48963214
6	Julie	26	Female	A+	12478963
7	Frank	35	Male	A-	85473216

LIKE

Like operator fetches records based on string matching. For instance if you want to select records of all patients whose name starts with 'J', you can use LIKE operator. The LIKE operator uses two wild cards for string matching. They are denoted by a percentage sign (%) and underscore sign (_). The % wild card specifies any number of characters whereas _ specifies only one character. So, if you want to fetch records of all the patients where name starts with J, you can use like operator as follows:

```
SELECT * FROM Patients

 WHERE name LIKE('J%')
```

Here you can see we use % wild card. Here 'J%' means that the name should start with J and after that there can be any number of characters. The output of this query will be:

id	name	age	gender	blood_group	phone
3	James	16	Male	O-	78452369
6	Julie	26	Female	A+	12478963

Similarly, if you want to select all the records where 'a' is the second character in the name, you can use '_' wildcard as follows:

```
SELECT * FROM Patients

 WHERE name LIKE('_a%')
```

Here '_a%' specifies that there can be one and only one character before character 'a' and after that there can be any number of characters. The output of this query will look like this:

id	name	age	gender	blood_group	phone
3	James	16	Male	O-	78452369
4	Matty	43	Female	B+	15789634
5	Sal	24	Male	O+	48963214
9	Hales	54	Male	B+	74698125

You can see, all the names have character 'a' in the second place.

DISTINCT

The DISTINCT selects only the distinct values from the specified column. For instance if you want to retrieve distinct patient ids from Patient_Examination table, you use DISTINCT operator as follows:

```
SELECT DISTINCT patient_id from Patient_Examination
```

IS NULL

IS NULL operator is used to retrieve those records where value for a particular column is NULL. A NULL value is used when we don't specify any value for the column. For instance if we want to retrieve records of all the patients where phone number is NULL, we can use following query:

```
SELECT * FROM Patients
 WHERE phone IS NULL
```

The above query will not retrieve any record, since there is no record in the Patients table where phone is NULL.

NEGATION Operators

Negation operators reverse the value of the operators used in conjunction with it. Following are the most commonly used negation operators in SQL.

- NOT NULL
- NOT IN
- NOT BETWEEN
- NOT LIKE

Let's see each of these negation operators in action.

NOT NULL

The NOT NULL operator fetches records where the column specified in the WHERE clause has no NULL values. The following query retrieves records of those patients whose phone is not NULL.

```
SELECT * FROM Patients
 WHERE phone IS NOT NULL
```

You will see all the records from the Patients table in the output since no record has NULL value in its phone column.

NOT IN

The NOT IN operator reverses the output of the IN operator. For instance if you want to retrieve records of all the patients except those with blood group O+ and O-, you can use NOT IN operator as follows:

```
SELECT * FROM Patients
 WHERE blood_group NOT IN('O+', 'O-')
```

The output will look like this:

id	name	age	gender	blood_group	phone
2	Kimer	45	Female	AB+	45686412
4	Matty	43	Female	B+	15789634
6	Julie	26	Female	A+	12478963
7	Frank	35	Male	A-	85473216
8	Alex	21	Male	AB-	46971235
9	Hales	54	Male	B+	74698125

NOT BETWEEN

Similarly NOT BETWEEN operators retrieverecords that do not fall between specified ranges. To retrieve records from the Patients table where id is not between 3 and 7, you can use NOT BETWEEN operator as follows:

```
SELECT * FROM Patients
 WHERE id NOT BETWEEN 3 and 7
```

The output of the above query will be:

id	name	age	gender	blood_group	phone
1	Tom	20	Male	O+	123589746
2	Kimer	45	Female	AB+	45686412
8	Alex	21	Male	AB-	46971235
9	Hales	54	Male	B+	74698125
10	Elice	32	Female	O+	34169872

NOT LIKE

Finally, the NOT LIKE operator retrieves those records that do not satisfy the criteria set by the LIKE operator.

For example, the following query retrieves records of all the patients who do not have 'a' as second character in their names.

```
SELECT * FROM Patients

 WHERE name NOT LIKE('_a%')
```

The above query will retrieve following records.

id	name	age	gender	blood_group	phone
1	Tom	20	Male	O+	123589746
2	Kimer	45	Female	AB+	45686412
6	Julie	26	Female	A+	12478963
7	Frank	35	Male	A-	85473216
8	Alex	21	Male	AB-	46971235
10	Elice	32	Female	O+	34169872

ORDER BY Clause

By default the data is retrieved in the order in which it was inserted. However you can sort the data according to some order. For instance you can sort the data by age, or alphabetically and so on. The ORDER BY clause is used for ordering data. Let's take a simple example of ORDER BY clause where data is sorted by age.

```
SELECT * FROM Patients
 ORDER BY age
```

In the output you will see that the records will be arranged by the ascending order of age. The output will look like this:

id	name	age	gender	blood_group	phone
3	James	16	Male	O-	78452369
1	Tom	20	Male	O+	123589746
8	Alex	21	Male	AB-	46971235
5	Sal	24	Male	O+	48963214
6	Julie	26	Female	A+	12478963
10	Elice	32	Female	O+	34169872
7	Frank	35	Male	A-	85473216
4	Matty	43	Female	B+	15789634
2	Kimer	45	Female	AB+	45686412
9	Hales	54	Male	B+	74698125

By default the data is arranged in the ascending order if the sorted column is integer and in alphabetical order if the sorting is implemented via string column. However, you can reverse the output of default sorting by adding DESC after the ORDER BY clause.

The following query retrieves records from the Patients table in reverse alphabetical order.

```
SELECT * FROM Patients
 ORDER BY name ASC
```

id	name	age	gender	blood_group	phone
8	Alex	21	Male	AB-	46971235
10	Elice	32	Female	O+	34169872
7	Frank	35	Male	A-	85473216
9	Hales	54	Male	B+	74698125
3	James	16	Male	O-	78452369
6	Julie	26	Female	A+	12478963
2	Kimer	45	Female	AB+	45686412

4	Matty	43	Female	B+	15789634
5	Sal	24	Male	O+	48963214
1	Tom	20	Male	O+	123589746

In this chapter we studied how we can filter records based on conditions. We also studied how to implement these conditions using operators and WHERE clause. Finally we covered how we can sort data in ascending and descending order using ORDER BY clause.

Conclusion

Well, we've come to the end. I hope you started this book as a somewhat intermediate-advanced user of SQL, and left, if not a better SQL developer, a better programmer.

If there was one takeaway I want you to have from this book, that is "SQL is a declarative language." It's been repeated throughout this book countless times, and yet still not enough.

Besides that, remember the importance of practice. It won't matter if you're an SQL prodigy if you don't put in the hours. Becoming a master at anything will take a huge amount of time, be it sewing or becoming an advanced web developer. Pour in the hours, and SQL's vast depths will reward you.

It's important to put in the necessary reps into theory before moving on to more complex practices.

In this book, we've also looked over the various prospects of SQL as a career path. Remember that if you find yourself not wanting to completely dedicate your life to becoming a web dev, that is not the end, nor have you wasted your time.

Your time learning SQL will have taught you a valuable skill which can be put to practice in a variety of jobs and positions, and most importantly, it taught you how to think. It's easy to underestimate the amount of impact that learning something complex like SQL can have on someone's thought process.

It's also very important to remember to exercise your brain properly. This is because not sleeping enough lets your brain cells deteriorate.

A balanced, healthy diet is also very important. Eating a lot of fish and seafood has proven benefits for the brain.

In the end, the most important thing to remember here is that almost everything is connected. The ability to exercise is as intimately connected to SQL as learning what a JOIN is.

If some parts of this book have been confusing, don't fret. That's a part of every programmer's learning curve. You can't just get out of bed one day and be a professional programmer working at Microsoft.

Try using the internet to help you out; online portals like Stack Overflow and similar have much more information than a single book ever could. Keep in mind not to use too many solutions from there, as it's quite a lazy practice and can mess you up professionally later. This is because the skill you'll be learning is not "Coding in SQL" it is "coding in Stack Overflow" and well, let's just say this book isn't about the latter.

Remember that these portals are resources, not all of your knowledge. This is another reason why you should learn the theoretical foundations behind SQL. The answers you find elsewhere won't mean much to you unless you have the necessary theoretical foundations to understand them fully.

For a second, I want to turn your eyes towards debugging. Yes, the most annoying part of coding, and yet so vital.

Debugging is actually one of the most marketable parts of coding, because to your boss, you'll seem like the guy that got what he asked for done, even if someone else wrote the code.

When it comes to debugging, look for common rookie mistakes. Missed calls, missed semicolons, improper joins and similar issues riddle the code of even seasoned professionals.

It's far too common for even seasoned developers to forget their reason for learning to code. Keeping that reason in mind is vital for pretty much every programmer's success. Similar to bodybuilders, if you lose sight of your reason, you might as well have lost sight of everything that made you an SQL developer.

When it comes to learning advanced programming techniques, this is doubly so. You will fail routinely. Chances are, you've failed multiple examples in this book, and yet you got up. It is that endurance, that drive to get up after failure that separates the mediocre developers from the cream of the crop.

If you simply want bragging rights, put that bragging in front of yourself and tunnel to it. Don't let anyone tell you that you can't, don't let them stop you.

If what you want is money, chase that cash. The worst thing that can happen to a developer is not forgetting all of their programming language know-how, but falling into decadence and forgetting why they're doing it in the first place.

It's natural to write buggy code, it's natural to want to fight the computer every time you try running your script. Instead of getting hung up on it, learn to improve.

Soon, you'll be running error-free, smooth scripts at your dream job. There's no limit to the vertical mobility a good developer can have. Even when the frustration and hopelessness feel almost unbearable, remind yourself of the feeling you get when your code finally runs. There are few better feelings in this world than your code working right the first time you run it.

With that said, it's always important to keep in mind the career prospects of SQL development. You will never have the risk of unemployment for long. With most other jobs, their employment rate grows at sub 10%, but in the US, programming jobs easily eclipse that by twice or more. This means that there'll always be companies looking for you, and that is an excellent feeling.

Heck, you can even go freelance! Rid yourself of the shackles presented to you by the corporate world and become your own boss. Find your own clients, run your own SQL-automated marketing campaigns. Don't let anything stop you until you're a true star developer.

If you need some encouragement, simply look at some freelancing sites like UpWork, look at who's making the most money there? Marketers and web developers. An excellent web developer can easily charge $100 an hour and always be booked out. And I don't mean "making ends meet". I mean, if they wanted to, they could work at 20 grand a month. Yes, 200,000 USD a year, or even more, is achievable from being a freelance developer.

This is not even counting the possibility of being employed at one of the best companies in the world. Google and Microsoft are always looking for competent, seasoned developers to join their ranks.

Because of all this professional viability, many people are electing to enter the world of web development. You, as an advanced reader, are a step in front of the rest, but if you want to stay competitive, you can't let them catch up.

You need to be constantly improving yourself, constantly working on your knowledge, expanding the areas you're an expert on.

While it may seem odd to recommend in a book about SQL, do learn some other languages. Pure SQL can be powerful, but it is a true beast when coupled with a good object-oriented language, in the hands of a competent programmer.

Don't shy away from markup languages like HTML and CSS either, they're really easy to learn and can boost your employability significantly.

Even if you don't end up going into programming, your knowledge of SQL will come in handy. For example, if you become a writer, you can make your own website, or as an artist, your own online portfolio. If you end up as a manager, you'll know how to speak to the web development team much better than anyone else there, ensuring you an easy promotion.

Learning advanced SQL is merely step one; you'll have to keep up with this pace for the rest of your professional career if you want to stay at the top.

Most importantly, remember to take breaks and relax. Don't tire yourself too much and end up burning out. This is what happens to many promising developers.

Keep working on what you enjoy, you should always have at least one passion project besides your job. It will help keep your love for programming and SQL alive.

So, to recoup everything said:

- Practice a lot, there's never enough hours put in.

- Keep yourself healthy, it helps your brain stay sharp.

- Always have a passion project to keep your interest high.

- Never stop improving.

- Learn a few other languages to complement your SQL knowledge.

- You can always switch careers easily, and freelancing is a very promising avenue if you're good enough.

And above all else, *make sure you love what you're doing* and don't burn out!

www.ingramcontent.com/pod-product-compliance
Lightning Source LLC
LaVergne TN
LVHW051226050326
832903LV00028B/2262